COMPUTER STUDIES

COURSEWORK COMPANION

Ray Bradley

GCSE

Charles Letts & Co Ltd
London, Edinburgh & New York

First published 1989
by Charles Letts & Co Ltd
Diary House, Borough Road, London SE1 1DW

Text: © Ray Bradley 1989
Cover photograph: Tom Tracy, Image Bank
Handwriting samples: Artistic License
Diagrams: Kevin Jones Associates
Cartoons: Michael Renouf
Photographs on page 66: Steffan Jones-Hughes (Textile designer)
Illustrations: © Charles Letts & Co Ltd 1989

British Library Cataloguing in Publication Data
Bradley, Ray, *1951*-
    GCSE computer studies. – (Letts coursework
    companion)
    1. Computer systems
    I. Title
    004

ISBN 0 85097 858 0

Printed and bound in Great Britain by
Charles Letts (Scotland) Ltd

Contents

Introduction to projects

Why we need to do projects

There are many types of skill that can't be tested properly in an exam. This is especially true for a practical subject like computer studies. In doing projects, you have the opportunity to show what you can do *during* the course, and not rely totally on the exam at the end. For many students who are worried about exams this is an added bonus. It is a great advantage for students who work hard during the course, or students who get nervous and don't always do their best in an exam.

What's special about computer studies projects?

There can be few subjects that offer the variety of projects that are available to computing students. This is especially true if your school is fortunate enough to have lots of good up-to-date equipment. You may find choosing what to do is a difficult task, though.

About this book

This book is not simply a collection of completed projects. Instead, it concentrates on how to go about thinking up ideas, solving common problems and showing many different types of project.

Don't get the wrong idea!

It's important to realize that, as many projects are to be shown, no single project can be in its *final* form.

Using this book

You should read the book at the end of the first year or the beginning of the second year of your GCSE course. You *could* read this book from the beginning to the end, but you may find this is *not* the best way for you.

To help find your way around quickly, consider the following.

Can't think of anything to do?

There is a long list of ideas at the end of Section Seven.

Need lots of general help and advice?

Then read Section Nine, which answers many of the questions that students often ask.

Stuck over complicated computer jargon?

Then look up the word in the glossary in Section Ten.

Thought of what to do but can't think how to start?

Then read Sections Three and Four.

Finished your project? Ready to write the documentation?

Then read Section Eight.

Thinking of using a software package for your project?

Then read Section Six.

Thinking of writing your own computer programs?

Then read Section Five.

Want to know what different type
of projects there are?

Then read Section Two.

This can be summarized as follows.

Section Two

This explains the different types of projects that you can do. *It is essential reading – before any other sections.*

Sections Three and Four

These cover the **analysis** and **design** sections of a single project in detail. *Read them to get an idea of how the initial stages can be developed, and the solution is found.*

Section Five

A completely different type of project is tackled. The special problems with a control project are outlined. *This is essential reading if your project might involve BASIC.*

Section Six

A problem is solved by making use of a number of different packages. Modern projects now tend to be of this type.

Section Seven

Many varied project ideas are covered in less detail. This is a section about ideas. It finishes off with a comprehensive list of possible project titles.

Section Eight

An important section about the project documentation. This section *must* be read to help you understand the project write-up.

Section Nine

A section giving lots of help and advice. *Essential reading.*

Section Ten

A glossary of project related terms. Some of the terms, e.g. 'satellite systems', are explained solely in the way they have been used in this book.

Types of hardware and software

There are many different types of computer used in schools. Don't be put off if your computer system is different from the ones in this book. It's the *ideas* that are important.

Types of project

Don't stop reading parts of the book that at first sight might not be catering for your interests. There will be lots of good ideas, hints and tips that could be useful for your project.

Organize your time wisely

You will need to be organized if you are to produce a good project in the time available. If you are doing a two year course then planning your project usually starts in the third term of the first year. This means that you can start practical work at the beginning of the second year.

Some students have the ability to start their projects early. Many students think they have! Don't start too early! You get better as you gain more experience.

Glossary of terms

It's important that you understand the special terms that are used in computer studies projects. These are described in the glossary in Section Ten. Don't skip over words that you don't understand. Refer to the glossary section, or if the word is not there, ask your teacher.

Checklists

In some sections there are checklists. These cover important points. When you are undertaking your own projects these checklists can be used to make sure that your project also has these points covered.

Different examination boards requirements

These are listed in the Syllabus Analysis, in Appendix 1.

What's it all about?

Different types of project

Until recently, all computer studies projects involved programming. Students had to think up ideas that they could solve using a language such as BASIC. With the introduction of the GCSE, and the vast amount of suitable applications packages, it is now possible to have a much more interesting range of projects to choose from.

People in industry would normally be given a problem to solve, using the best means they have. They could write their own programs or, more likely, use **applications packages** (special software such as **databases**).

At school you would be expected to take a similar approach. Take care, though, and check what you are letting yourself in for! It may be best not to choose certain types of project, for example, it would be silly to choose a problem that requires programming if you hate writing your own programs. In this book there are different types of project. In the end, your project may end up using several of these methods.

What types of project are there?

Consider four different types of project.

Project type 1: Using an applications software package

Suppose you have a simple database available, and you wish to design a system that will help someone on a diet to plan their meals.

Baked beans might have the following entry:

Baked beans	Typical values/100 g
energy	65 kcal
protein	5.2 g
carbohydrate	11.2 g
total fat	0.4 g
dietary fibre	7.3 g

You might decide to offer a printout of total calories for the day for someone on a calorie controlled diet, or a printout of the total fat consumed in a day for someone prone to heart disease, etc. Perhaps you could include options to list all foods that have less than 200 calories for a typical portion, or make a list of special menus. You could even list the vitamins added as well.

Don't waste time trying to write a complex program. Instead, make use of the database package to help solve the problem more simply. You will then have time to make the final solution more useful.

The above example, if written in BASIC from scratch, would be a project for a whizz-kid! By using the database package, though, you should be able to make a final system that is very good indeed.

To be interested in this type of project you need to *like* the topic that you have chosen. Otherwise, you will soon become bored. Also, try to ensure that you produce a package that is *useful*. The home economics department at your school would probably be interested in an idea like the one above.

If you can't think of what to do yourself, ask people who teach your favourite subjects to come up with some ideas. Don't limit yourself to teachers at school, though. Ask your parents, friends and business people if they can help.

If you find a problem that can make use of more than one package, then this will be an added bonus, as you are likely to gain more marks. Section Three shows a project that makes use of a database package and a word processor.

Project type 2: Writing your own programs

Don't write a basic program if this is not the best solution.

There are thousands of application packages for computers, but you will have access to only a few of them. You may actually enjoy writing your own programs, especially if you are good at it.

If you are going to write a program for a project then you need to put in a lot of *extra work* learning features of the language that are *not taught in class*. A large part of your coursework will involve finding out things for yourself. This is usually done by reading the manuals for the computer system you are using.

If you are good at and enjoy programming, then this is a good choice of project, but don't discount software packages altogether, as it's usually possible to choose a much more interesting project, using them. Also, and this is very important, you *must* think carefully about the *problem* you are trying to solve. *Is it really best solved by writing a program?* If not, you would be unwise to use that particular problem for your programming project.

When you think up ideas for your programs try and be original. The moderators can get tired of quiz programs. They have been chosen so often before that they are becoming boring and tedious to mark. Instead, what about a special teaching program that would be really useful for primary school children? How about something for handicapped children who can't use a computer keyboard? What about people who can't read? All these ideas, if developed with the help of specialist staff, can produce excellent material for programming projects.

The new Bodgem package only takes three minutes .....

Try to find someone with a special need, and see if you can write a program to help out. It not only makes a good project but helps you to increase your experience. But beware! Don't choose a project that is too difficult, or you will not help *anybody*. Discuss it carefully with your computer studies teacher before agreeing to do anything.

Project type 3: Modifying existing software

This type of project involves changing a system that somebody else has already set up. Suppose that last year a student had written a simple library cataloguing system. It may be your task to add some routines to enable library staff to use the computer to keep a check on books taken from the library.

Don't try to modify badly written programs.

It is most important that any software that you intend to modify is **very well written** and **documented**. Otherwise, your task will be almost impossible. It would be quicker to start again from scratch. (Then you would not be doing this type of project!)

Any software that you intend to modify must have been written with this in mind at the beginning. You should realize from your computing lessons that large programs should always be split up into **modules**. Each module is then called up by a simple **main routine**. All that should be necessary is to write some additional routines and *call* them from the main module. If this does not apply to the software you intend to modify, don't attempt it at all.

Many excellent projects can be developed over the years by groups of students adding to the basic ideas. As long as all the early students undertake their part of the project properly, then later students should be able to cope. Indeed, small businesses have been set up by computing students working in schools as teams. **Organization** and **excellent documentation** are the keys to this type of project – and most others. It will almost certainly be the case that a teacher has started a project and overseen the groups of students over a period of several years.

Project type 4: A control project

How about designing an automatic customer counting system? You could think about a system that counts the number of supporters for each team going into a football stadium, or fans going into a rock concert.

Your project could be to build some simple turnstiles (perhaps using Technic Lego or Fischertechnik), and then interface them to the computer. You would then have to write a control program to work out things like:
- how many supporters for each team there were at the match
- how much money was taken

etc. Think about producing statistics showing how many supporters were at the match each week.

Don't spend too long building the hardware.

Note that the building of the **hardware** is only a minor part of the project. Most of the marks are awarded for the **software** and **documentation**. Therefore, the hardware must be simple and quick to construct. Many students in the past have built complex circuits only to find that there is no time left to do any useful software. If your project write-up is poor, then few marks will be awarded, even if you build a superb working robot! Don't fall into this trap!

Are there any other projects?

All projects really fall into one of the categories noted above. The variety of projects is limited only by your imagination, ability, available equipment and time. For example, consider the first category using an applications software package. In this category alone there are:
- *databases*
- *word processors*
- *spreadsheets*
- *computer aided design packages*
- *stock control systems*
- *viewdata systems*
- *music systems*
- *computer art packages*
- *desk top publishing systems*

and many others.

Section Seven of this book contains well over 50 project ideas for you to use.

Choosing your project type

You should have a good idea of what types of project there are. It is important that you make the right choice at an early stage. You can't easily change your mind later, especially if much time and effort have already been put into your project.

Perhaps the problem that you have chosen could be a combination of programming and packages. You really *do* need to consider the problem and, given your resources at school or college, choose the best methods from what you have. Don't choose a problem just to fit your method of solution! However, *and this is just as important,* don't choose a problem that is likely to result in a method of solution that you hate. Ask your teacher for advice on these points.

Keep some different projects up your sleeve

"Don't choose a project that someones else is doing."

Finally, think up several different possible projects that you could do. This is important as your teacher may reject your first idea on grounds that you may not have considered. For example, you may have come up with a brilliant idea; you go to your teacher and are told that someone else in another class is already doing the same thing. It is *most unwise* to have the same projects from the same school or college in the same year.

✔ Checklist

1 There are several major types of project:
(a) making use of software packages
(b) writing your own programs
(c) modifying existing software
(d) control programs
2 All projects involve finding out much more than you are taught during lesson times.
3 Try choosing a project which is useful to somebody.
4 If you are going to modify existing software, make sure that you fully understand the old software before starting the project.
5 Don't undertake control projects unless you know what you are doing or can get specialist help.
6 The best solution to your chosen problem may be a combination of different types of solutions.
7 Choose the best computer solution to your project, but don't choose a problem which may lead to a method of solution which you don't like.
8 Have several ideas ready before making any final decision.

Starting a project
(an example)

In the beginning . . .

Everybody starts off with a blank piece of paper! Trying to think of what to do can be tricky. Most people tend to get ideas from their hobbies. Some get excellent ideas from the work experience they have done, or Saturday jobs they might have. Often, there is a wealth of ideas you can get from different teachers at school.

Having thought of a problem you think might be suitable, what do you do next? The whole idea of this section is to put you *on the right track*. The example used is unimportant. How you go about the analysis of the problem (any problem) is *very important*. *Your* project might be a lot simpler than the one shown, but the ideas will be the same.

The initial ideas

Let's suppose that after speaking with one of your teachers you become interested in getting the computer automatically to print out end-of-term reports. (Perhaps you can secretly get it to give you an excellent one!)

Find out some more information

The first thing to do is arrange an interview with the teacher concerned, and decide exactly what is needed. Don't forget to think up some suitable questions *before* the interview. Write them down so that you don't forget them. Make notes *during* the interview. You could tape record the interview if the teacher does not object. You should be able to borrow a cassette tape recorder if you don't have one.

Let's suppose that the following major points came out of the interview:

Interview notes (not in any special order)

(a) To make things easy, we shall write reports only on **information technology** courses.

(b) The teacher writes reports once a term. Each term there is a major theme; these are:

- term 1   introduction and word processing
- term 2   desk top publishing and art packages
- term 3   CAD and a multiple-choice test on the years work.

(c) The teacher needs the option of looking at the reports on screen before they are printed.

(d) There are never more than 200 students in the third year at any time.

(e) The report writing should be as automatic as possible. Ideally, the teacher should be able to type 'REPORT', walk away for a few hours, then come back and pick up a pile of reports ready to give out to the parents!

(f) Typing in data about each student should be quick and easy. **Verification** and **validation** should be carried out if possible. (You should know these two important words!)

Keep a diary. Start it early.

(g) Typing in new students' details each year should also be quick and easy. Again, verification and validation should be carried out whenever possible.

(h) The computer should be able to check the spelling in each report before the report is printed out. This includes the spellings of forenames and surnames for each student.

Keeping a diary

It is **essential** that you keep some sort of record *at all stages of your project*. This need not be a nuisance, rough notes made now will be of great help during the later stages of your work. Any good ideas that you have, or any problems that crop up, should all be put in your diary.

Typical diary entry for the above

The following is an example of what could go into your diary after the above interview.

Mon Nov 16th 1992

Had interview with the information technology teacher. Decided on a simple start with the third year IT only. The next stage is to get the project idea passed by my computer studies teacher. See interview notes in my project folder for more details.

What next? You can now go to your computer teacher and discuss possible ways of looking at the problem in more detail. Your teacher will know what systems the school has, and therefore be able to suggest several different ways you could possibly solve the problem. This is usually called the **analysis** of the problem. The ways available to you will depend on the hardware and software packages that you can use.

The analysis of the problem

Assume that the idea has been passed by your teacher. Assume also that you have had another interview with the original teacher and drawn up a **specification** (a detailed list of what the system must do).

Don't lose out on the marks!

It is most important at this stage to look at the **marking scheme** for your examination board. Then write your **project specification** according to that marking scheme.

Some boards may not have a specific marking scheme, but they will have methods of giving you marks according to what you have done. For example, have you considered any alternatives? Have you justified your final choice? Have you mentioned any limitations, etc? Many students lose marks because they miss out so much vital information.

Make sure you produce a detailed specification.

The Northern Examining Association requires that the analysis-and-design sections be marked at an early stage. This means that you say what you are going to do and how you are going to do it *before* you start working on the computers. In this way you can't cheat and change the specification later!

A simple example of working with the marking scheme

Consider the Southern Examining Group's section for the definition of the problem. You get a maximum of six marks for this section which must include the following:

- a statement putting the problem into context
- a statement of the required results

- a description of the information needed to provide the required results
- a statement of the assumptions made and limitations recognized by the candidate in solving the problem.

The above sounds a little complicated. Basically, it can be summed up as follows.

Marks can range from one to two out of six if you show only a little understanding. To get five or even six out of six, you have to give a very good, well set out definition of your problem.

Special notes

Don't forget that when you read some of the following text, you must put yourself in the position of a person who is reading the report for the first time and knows nothing about what you are going to do. This is well worth remembering all the way through your project work.

A good definition of the student report problem might be as follows.

An automatic report generation system

(i) Definition of the problem to be solved

The present manual system

At present the information technology teacher writes out the students' end of term reports by hand. This is a time-consuming and tedious task, as the teacher takes about 150 students for the same lessons for only one period per week. A typical report for an imaginary student is shown in Figure 3.1.

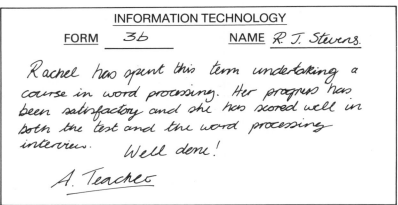

Fig. 3.1 The present manual reporting system

Using the present manual method, the teacher would have to record each student's marks in a mark book, add them up at the end of the term and work out whether the student had passed or failed. In addition to this, suitable comments are made about the student's attitude and effort for the term.

The proposed new computerized system

The new system will print out *automatically* standard reports for students who are studying information technology. Different major themes are undertaken each term. Briefly these are:
- term 1   word processing
- term 2   desk top publishing and art packages
- term 3   CAD and a multiple-choice test.

The teacher will supply information such as 'comments on attitude' and 'percentage marks'. The computer will then build up a report by using this and other information, such as surname and form, already stored in the computer. The computer will also check on the spellings of names and teacher's comments before the reports are printed.

If the system is successful, a considerable amount of valuable time will be saved. If the reports contain statements about what the students have been doing, then more useful and detailed reports can be presented to the parents. Writing in detail about what the students have done would normally be too time-consuming in the manual system. The same thing would have to be written out about 150 times!

(ii) Results expected from the system

A typical report for a pupil in word processing might be as shown in Figure 3.2. At present, a form pre-printed with INFORMATION TECHNOLOGY, FORM and NAME is used. The new system also needs to make use of these pre-printed standard size forms.

INFORMATION TECHNOLOGY

FORM . . . 3b   NAME . . . Stevens. R.J.

WORD PROCESSING MODULE FOR THE CERTIFICATE OF COMPETENCE IN INFORMATION TECHNOLOGY

Rachel has spent this term undertaking a course in word processing. Her attitude this term has been excellent. During her word processing test she scored 89% and during her word processing interview she showed an excellent mastery of the system.

At the end of the year we shall be awarding certificates to successful candidates and Rachel has reached DISTINCTION standard during the word processing part of the course.

Very well done indeed.

A. Teacher

Fig. 3.2 A typical example report for the first term

(iii) Information needed to produce the results

When the above word processing report is looked at in detail, it can be seen that only certain parts of the report change. These are:

(a) form (e.g. 3b)

(b) initials and surname (e.g. Stevens R.J.)

(c) first name (e.g. Rachel)

(d) attitude comment (e.g. excellent)

(e) word processing mark (e.g. 89%)

(f) word processing interview comment (e.g. showed an excellent mastery of the system)

(g) grade for the certificate (e.g. DISTINCTION)

(h) general remark at the end of the report (e.g. Very well done indeed.)

(i) finally, the sex of the pupil must also be known. This enables her or him, or she or he to be used in the right places.

In addition to the above, which must be stored for each student, there is the report text to store. The reports for the other terms, together with information **(d)** to **(h)** will be different.

To sum up, a database system must be built up consisting of all the surnames, forenames and forms for all the students in the third year. Three sets of comments and marks will also have to be stored for each student These correspond to each terms work. Finally, the text for each term's report must also be stored.

(iv) Some limitations of the system

(a) There will be a maximum capacity of 200 students.

(b) The style of the reports will all be very similar.

(c) The comments will be limited in length or they will not fit conveniently onto the report form.

 **Checklist**

You will see that the following very important points have been covered.

From part (i)

1 The **problem** that you want to solve using the computer is stated so that anybody can tell exactly what you are trying to do.

2 The **person** who will be using the system is mentioned. This is important because it gives the examiner an idea of how to judge your **user documentation** which comes later.

3 We have shown **why** the problem would be better tackled by computer rather than using the present manual method. There's not much point in trying to solve a problem that would be best done without a computer.

From part (ii)

4 The **output** required from the system is shown. Just one specific example is given here. Your project may require more than this.

From part (iii)

5 The **data** that has to be collected to be used in the report is shown in detail. These are the **inputs** to the system. Ways of getting this data into suitable forms will be shown in Section Four.

6 The **processing** that has to be done on the input data to produce the output data can now be seen. The methods available to do this are covered in Section Four.

Important things to note

When do I get to use the computer?

Lots of thought is needed before jumping on the computer.

You can see the amount of thought that has already gone into the project. If this stage is done well, then fewer problems should arise in the later stages. *Note that you have not yet touched a computer!* This comes very much later. You must *never* switch on the computer immediately and start programming. This is *not* the way to go about solving problems. You have not even decided if you are going to write any programs or use pre-written software packages yet. This comes in the next section.

Gosh! I didn't realize that!

It is important to realize that many marks are awarded for the **analysis** of the project, the **design** of the project (see later), and also for the **documentation**. Only about 20 per cent of the marks are for the actual program or the detailed methods of solution. This means that more effort should be put into specification, analysis, design and documentation than should be put into 'playing' on the computer. If you learn this one simple fact you will be a much wiser student.

What about different ways of solving the problem?

Some boards may want you to describe the possible ways in which you intend to carry out the project in this section. i.e. the design of the solution to the problem. Don't worry about this, it is included in Section Four.

Summary

1 Think of a good idea (read other sections in this book if you have not got one yet).

2 Try to think of a project that will be useful to someone.

3 Make sure that the person (or people) who will be using the project are consulted before you start. Arrange an interview if necessary.

4 Make some helpful notes before the interview.

5 Tape the interview or make notes during it.

6 Keep all these notes in your project diary.

7 Draw up a detailed specification of what you intend to do. Don't forget to write it such that a stranger who does not know what you are doing can understand.

8 Your board may want to be given the following details:

(a) who the user will be

(b) a description of the present manual methods

(c) the output required from the system

(d) the inputs needed to produce the outputs

(e) the processing that is going to be necessary

(f) the possible methods of solution with reasons for choice.

Note **(e)** and **(f)** are covered in Section Four.

9 Remember the golden rule:
Follow the marking scheme for your board.

10 Remember many marks can be obtained by doing some good analysis.

11 Don't switch on the computer and start working straight away. This comes much later and does not even make up most of the marks!

Designing the solution

The best way to get the job done

Having looked at a problem and produced a specification (see Section Three), you now need to find the best way of solving the problem. The student report system will be used once more and you should refer to Section Three if you are not familiar with it.

The key to the whole problem of the student report system is finding a suitable method of retrieving information and printing it out. From your computer studies lessons you will be aware of what an **information retrieval package** (database) is, and how information can be got from it.

This type of problem is difficult to solve using BASIC. As a GCSE programming exercise it would be far too complicated. You can therefore assume that the only easy way is to make use of *pre-written* software packages.

An important idea to consider for this system is the use of an **integrated software package**. That is, the database must be able to share information with systems such as word processors and spelling checkers etc. The school's standard word processing and database software may well have this facility.

The hardware and software

Decide on the software and hardware you will use.

In your project you will have to specify the exact hardware and software that you will use. It would be unusual if you had more than a few systems to choose from. Nevertheless, if you have, and can say why a particular package or system would be better, then marks can be gained more easily.

None of it's any good! I don't believe it!!

If the software that you have available seems to be inadequate, see your project supervisor immediately. It could simply be that you do not know enough about the systems that are available. If, in the end, you really *can't* solve the problem, then you will have to choose another project.

An example set-up (configuration)

One suggested configuration with all the required facilities is:

- **BBC Master 128** computer with two local dual-sided 5¼″ disc drives and ADFS filing system.

Using this filing system each disc drive is capable of storing about 655K bytes of information.

The computer has 128K of RAM, and supports the BBC BASIC language. There is a resident word processor called **View**.

- **Acornsoft View** word processor, with **printer driver**.
- **Acornsoft Viewstore** database package, which allows data to be passed to the View word processor.
- **Beebugsoft spelling checker**, which checks the spelling of any View word processor text.
- **Brother dot matrix printer** with single sheet feed mechanism. (Printer also has NLQ mode.)

Split up your problem into inputs, outputs, and processing.

So how do you intend using all this?

You now have to outline the steps in your proposed solution. This can be done in many ways, but it is often useful to split the problems into sub-sections. As always, **input**, **output** and **processing** are good starting points.

Don't forget you are playing the role of **systems analyst**.

The problems of input

Data capture form

The information technology teacher needs to enter a lot of data, for example, surname, comments and marks. You must design a convenient way in which data can be entered quickly and, if possible, be checked.

Validation

If possible, always validate the data.

It's easy to validate some of the data. The marks for a test are very easy as they must lie between 0 and 100 per cent. Letters or numbers outside this range would be rejected.

It should also be possible to validate some of the comments. For example, you might limit them to words like *excellent*, *good*, *average* or *poor*.

The key to being able to validate the data is knowing its type, e.g. **text** or **numeric**, and knowing its **range** (list of possible values its can take).

Length for each item of data

Some data will have to be limited in length. For example, you might decide to limit the surname and initials to 25 characters. This sort of information is shown in Table 4.1 below.

Data	Abbreviation	Data type	Max. length	Example
Surname and Initials	SURNAME	text	25	BOND J.
First name	FIRSTNAME	text	15	James
Form	FORM	alphanumeric	3	3a
House	HOUSE	text	2	WH
Sex	SEX	text	1	M

Table 4.1 Data specification

The data to be typed in by the teacher

The initial information to be typed in at the start of the term, together with its abbreviation, data type, length and examples are given in Table 4.1.

More validation can be done

Suppose there are ten houses in the school. The abbreviations for the houses are Sc, PS, JH, FH, PH, MH, HS, WH, SH and WW. Combinations of letters other than these will therefore be rejected at the validation stage.

Similarly, the only forms allowed will be 3a, 3b, 3c, 3d, 3e1 and 3e2, and the only sex allowed will be M or F.

During the first term, the data for the word processing course would have to be typed in. This is shown in Table 4.2.

Data	Abbreviation	Data type	Max. length	Example
Word processing percentage mark	WOR%	numeric	3	85
Word processing comment	WPCOMMENT	text	12	excellent
Word processing interview comment	WPICOMMENT	text	12	adequate
Grade for test	GRADE1	text	11	DISTINCTION
General comment for first term	GENCOMMENT1	text	50	Very well done.

The **grade** is based upon the following:

0 to 59%	FAIL
60% to 74%	PASS
75% to 84%	CREDIT
85% to 100%	DISTINCTION

Table 4.2 Data for the first term

If possible, the database system could generate the grade by checking to see if the marks entered were in the above range. It could then automatically store the grade to save the teacher typing it in.

During the second term, the data for the desk top publishing course would be entered. This might be as in Table 4.3.

Data	Abbreviation	Data type	Max. length	Example
Desk top publishing %	DTP%	numeric	3	72
DTP comment	DTPCOMMENT	text	12	good
DTP interview comment	DTPICOMMENT	text	12	poor
Grade for test	GRADE2	text	11	CREDIT
General comment for second term	GENCOMMENT2	text	50	A good term's work. Well done.

Table 4.3 Data for the second term

Finally, during the third term, the data for the computer aided design course may be as in Table 4.4.

Data	Abbreviation	Data type	Max. length	Example
Computer aided design %	CAD%	numeric	3	34
CAD comment	CADCOMMENT	text	12	average
CAD interview comment	CADICOMMENT	text	12	inadequate
Grade for test	GRADE3	text	11	PASS
General comment for third term	GENCOMMENT3	text	50	A disappointing term. Must work harder.
Multiple choice test mark	MUL%	numeric	3	0

Table 4.4 Data for the third term

File design

When setting up any database package you will need to supply special information so that the package can set up the files. Having seen what data has to be entered, this is now very easy. For example, there will be a *maximum of 200 records*, i.e. the system will cope until you have more than two hundred students in third year. (The specification on page 21 said that this will never happen.)

Each **record** must have a **key field** by which the record will be known. SURNAME is the obvious choice for our system – although care may be needed in case of twins!

Each record must then be split up into **fields**, and each field contains information about the student whose name is given in the **key field**. The information for each field was given in the above tables (i.e. the **data** column for each table).

File size

The size of the file needed can be worked out by adding up the maximum number of characters required for each student, then multiplying by 200.

Field	Max. size
Surname	25
Forename	15
Form	3
⋮	⋮
Multiple choice test mark	3
Total bytes/student	**313**

(Make sure you agree with this total by adding up all 'max. length' columns in the tables.)

Now make it a nice round figure – say 350.

Hence, size of file will be $200 \times 350 = 70\,000$ bytes.

This means that it will easily fit on the 650K disc.

Data capture form design

It can be seen that apart from the names, form, sex and house, there are three similar sections. The screen can thus be split up into three natural parts. Only one part needs to be seen at any time.

The screen can be laid out in any way that you wish. A convenient way for the first term is shown in Figure 4.1.

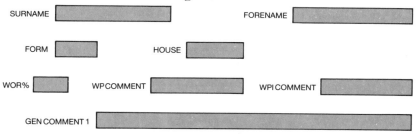

Fig. 4.1 Data capture screen for the first term

The system must be set up so that all the validation is carried out as the data is being entered.

Verification

The only practical way to verify the data is to check manually that each name, house, mark etc has been entered correctly. For example, there is no easy way to check that 67 has been entered instead of 77 for a specific mark. Similarly, there is no easy way to check that a name should be spelt 'Stephen' instead of 'Steven', other than by asking the student and manually checking.

What happens if it goes wrong?

Always assume that things will go wrong!

Oh no! I've lost the disc!

It would be drastic if any of the above data were to get lost through a faulty disc or carelessness etc. It is therefore **essential** that at least one back-up copy (and preferably more) is kept on a separate disc in a separate place to the working copy. Whenever a significant amount of data is added, then a new back-up disc should be made.

Bother! the power's gone!

The suggested database writes the data to disc at frequent intervals. Therefore, if there *were* to be a power cut, only the last one or two data entries would be lost. This should not be a problem.

A systems flowchart for the data entry system is shown in Figure 4.2.

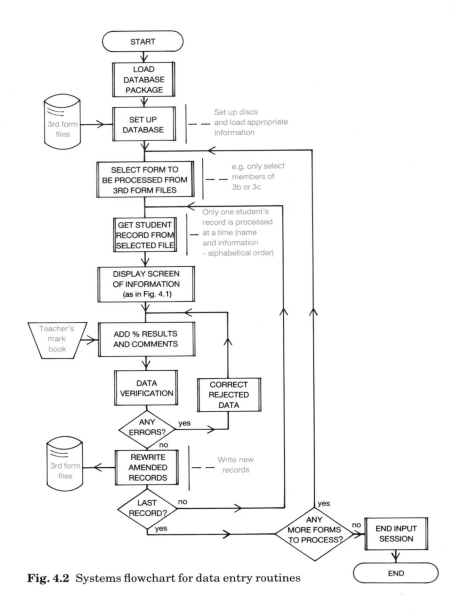

Fig. 4.2 Systems flowchart for data entry routines

As the spelling of each report must be checked before printing, then a word processor must be used to produce the output. It is intended that a standard letter approach be used. The word processor can do this by

Look at the report on page 21 to see how easy the idea is.

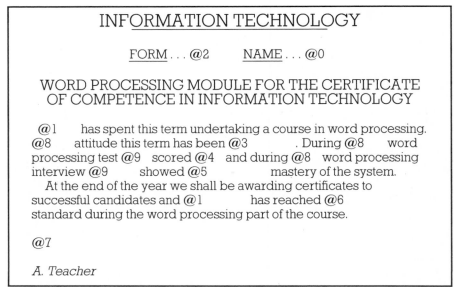

Fig. 4.3 Standard letter for first term's report

making use of **macros**. The **standard text** (i.e. text that does not change) is entered into the word processor and saved on disc. The file can then be spell checked. When a different comment or mark is needed, a **macro parameter** can be used instead. This sounds complicated but is, in fact, quite simple.

The idea is shown in Figure 4.3, and should be compared with the actual report generated on page 21.

The '@' signs (parameters) are used by the computer and replaced with the items listed in Table 4.5.

Parameter	To be replaced by
@0	Surname and initials
@1	First name
@2	Form
@3	Attitude for term
@4	Word processing percentage mark
@5	Word processing interview comment
@6	Grade
@7	General comment number 1
@8	her/his
@9	she/he

Table 4.5 Parameters

A systems flowchart for the **output** section is shown in Figure 4.4.

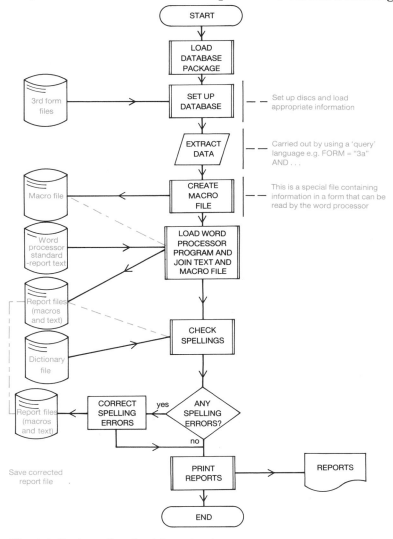

Fig. 4.4 Systems flowchart for output

The processing

Fortunately, all the technical details of the processing are taken care of by the software package. This was the main reason for doing it this way rather than writing your own programs.

As with most databases, to carry out processing you need to go through a 'question and answer' session. This usually instructs the package to **search** for certain items of data based on special **search criteria**. You may, for example, wish to find all the boys in Welldon House (WH) who have reached distinction standard. You may then want to instruct the package to print out, or produce a file, in alphabetical order, of information such as boys' names together with the actual marks that were awarded.

The main advantage of using a database is that, if the information is *in* it, you can usually specify exactly what you want *out*, and *how* it is to be arranged.

For the purposes of this project, a sensible request would be to print out all the reports for students in 3c. You would have to instruct the computer to produce a file with all the appropriate parameters in it. These parameters would have to be in the correct order, and ready to be used by the word processor. The standard letter as described earlier (see page 21) would be used.

Typical example of building a file

Search criteria needed
FORM = 3c

Parameters to be extracted from each record

@0	Surname and initials
@1	First name
@2	Form
@3	Attitude for term
@4	Word processing percentage mark
@5	Word processing interview comment
@6	Grade
@7	General comment number 1
@8	her/his
@9	she/he

You need to decide whether to include her/his and she/he in the actual database itself. If they are included, then the teacher will have to type them in, and another two fields will be needed. There will not be a problem of space but it will be tedious for the teacher. There must be a way to obtain this information from the sex of the pupil which is already known. This type of problem will be looked at in the **implementation** stage.

Important point to note

Imagine the extra work you would have if the above problem was only noticed after the database had been set up! This is a good example of why we have so much **analysis** and **design** before we attempt to set the system up on the computer.

A typical systems flowchart for the setting up section is shown in Figure 4.5.

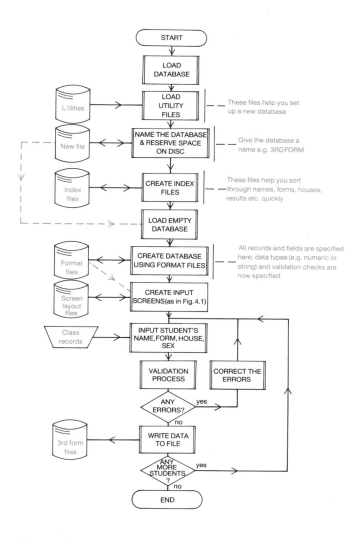

Fig. 4.5 Systems flowchart for setting up

Checklist

1 You are thinking how to computerize the system. You are not going to write a program because it would be too complicated for this problem.

2 Make sure that you have listed the exact hardware and software that you intend to use for your project.

3 Make sure that you cover input, processing and output in your design section.

4 Make sure that you have shown how you will **validate** all possible items of data that are entered into your system.

5 Make sure you have given enough information about the design of your files.

6 Make sure that you have designed a **data capture form** and shown if any of your data can be **verified**.

7 Make sure that you have allowed for **recovery from errors** in your systems analysis.

8 Make sure you have covered the **output** section, including the exact form that the output will take.

9 Have you got a detailed **algorithm** to show what processing will be necessary (i.e. showing exactly how it will be done)?

Is there any more?

In Sections Three and Four all the detailed **analysis** and **design** stages have been covered. Note that you have still not used the computer yet! This comes in the **implementation** and **testing** stages later.

It would take another two sections to cover these properly, plus another section on documentation. However, to make the book more useful we shall leave this project and go on to other types of project in the next sections. Don't forget that the *subject* of this example, the student reporting system, was itself unimportant. The *way that we have tackled* the problem is common to many different problems and is very important.

Summary

1 You must decide if pre-written software packages are to be used, or if you will write your own programs. You must have valid reasons for your choice.

2 If you are to write your own programs you must decide which language you will use, and why.

3 Make a list of the possible **hardware** and **software** that you could use for solving your problems.

4 Never assume that the person who marks your project is familiar with the packages you are using.

5 Choose the systems that you will use. It is most important to say why one system is, in your opinion, better than the others you could have chosen.

6 Split the **design** of the system into **inputs**, **outputs** and **processing**. Then produce **algorithms** to show how each will be solved.

7 For the **inputs** consider:
- the data capture form
- validation
- verification
- disasters (e.g. corrupt disc, power cut etc).

Draw a **systems flowchart** or **structure diagram** for the input section.

8 For the **outputs** consider:
- detailed design of the output
- what data is needed to produce this output.

Draw a **systems flowchart** or **structure diagram** for the output section.

9 For the **processing** consider:
- what has to be done with the input data to produce the output data.
- produce a detailed algorithm if necessary.

This can take the form of a **systems flowchart** or **structured diagram** or simply groups of statements saying how the problem may be solved.

10 All of this work can be done *without* using the computer. Make sure that you don't fall into the trap of using the computer at the start of your project before you have really thought about and analysed the problem.

A sample project

The best way to get the job done

We could continue with details of how the students' report problem in Sections Three and Four could be successfully solved. However, to give more variety we shall choose a completely different project for this section. Please read this section carefully, especially if you think you are going to use programming in your project. It contains many helpful hints and tips.

The new project

You have decided to use a computer in your home to make it look as if the house is occupied when you are out or on holiday. It will also act as a burglar alarm during these periods, and during the night when the house is occupied but people are asleep.

The specification

Assume that, after much thought, the following specification has been drawn up.

(a) Four lights are to be independently controlled. These are in the lounge, kitchen, main bedroom and bathroom.

(b) All external windows and doors are to be monitored. If any is opened during the times when the alarm system is active a bell will operate.

(c) It must be possible to switch the system off instantly by the press of a button.

(d) The system must be capable of operating without attention until different alarm times need to be set.

(e) The times during which the alarm system is active should be easily changed if necessary by someone who is not a computer specialist.

Limitations of the system

Produce a detailed specification with some limitations of your project.

(a) Assume that the same cycle will be gone through each day. This will make the project more simple.

(b) If the alarm sounds and nobody is in, then it will continue to sound for a period of five minutes and stop. If this happens, assume that the house has been burgled. In this case (assuming that the computer has not been stolen!) the system will have to be reset manually.

(c) If a power cut occurs then the system will fail. Battery back-up could be made available but this would be too complicated for the purpose of this project.

(d) A simple model of a house will be used for demonstration and testing of the project.

The systems

These are selected following the procedures in Section Four. The BASIC language will probably be used as most micros have an easy way to let BASIC switch electrical devices on and off.

The computer would not be able to control an actual house unless a competent electrician wired up the system. For the purpose of the GCSE project, a simulated house would be used. Instead of mains voltages, a circuit with small 5 V bulbs will be used.

A small model of the house, with suitable doors and windows, can be made from wood and glue. If an old dolls' house could be found then this would be ideal.

You should be able to get help from CDT departments at school. Don't forget to ask for help politely. Remember that these teachers will be busy with their own GCSE projects, so keep your requests simple and do the work yourself. Ask only for guidance.

The system described above is also ideal for software development. There's not much point in developing the software on an actual house. Imagine the chaos caused by the alarm going on and off at all times of the day and night if the system goes wrong!

Some new problems

(But don't be put off by them!)

One problem that this type of project presents is that of convincing the project moderator that it works. It is not really feasible to send a dolls' house through the post! You would also be assuming that the moderator has the same type of computer as you.

Identify any special problems with your type of problems.

The best option open to you is to make a short VHS video presentation, but check with the board first, to see if they will accept videos. If not, or if you do not have access to a video camera, then photographs can be just as good.

Make sure that you *can do* these extras, such as the model and the video. Otherwise you should not undertake this type of project. Concentrate *most* effort on the computing problems and *not* on the construction of the house or making your Spielberg movie! Even if you decide to avoid this type of project do read on. The way that the problems are solved is common to many programming and other projects.

How do we start? Structure diagrams and flowcharts are useful methods to help you start sorting out how problems can be solved.

Write 'Computer-controlled house' in a box as shown in Figure 5.1(a). You have now started! Next think up suitable ways of splitting the problem up into sub-problems. For example: **Make house**, **Documentation** and **Software** are some of the possibilities. This is shown in Figure 5.1(b).

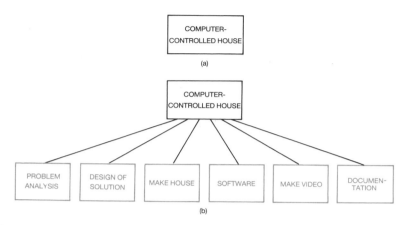

Fig. 5.1 How do we start?

How do we start writing the software?

As before, the thing *not* to do is get straight onto the computer! (Frustrating isn't it!) Lots of thought must be put into splitting the problem into several much smaller, easier ones. This is called **analysing** the problem.

Any system usually has **inputs** and **outputs**. Can you identify them for this one? Once the inputs and outputs are sorted out, the **processing** that needs to be done can be decided.

Inputs to the system

(a) The data that is entered by the user to control the on-off times of the alarm.

(b) The **reset** or **panic** button to switch the system off.

(c) The signal from the doors and windows to tell the computer that one of them has been opened.

Outputs from the system

(a) The four signals to control the lights.

(b) The signal to control the alarm bell.

(c) Probably a screen display showing the state of the alarm system.

Any computer studies project can be split up into inputs, outputs, and processing.

What next?

Once the inputs and outputs have been sorted out you can get on with the processing. You will be amazed at how easily this falls into place once these simple tasks have been carried out. As an example, consider the problem of entering the data.

First you have to get the data into the system to control the alarm. This will probably be in the form of on and off times etc.

You will have to decide on a typical day to test the system. Part of the day might be as shown in Table 5.1. The comments show the sort of simulation that you need to create. Therefore, you will have to design a system that enables the user to input suitable data. It would be sensible to have a standard table of values which will always be used unless the user wants to change things. These could be called the **default values** (a term with which you should be familiar).

Time	Lounge	Kitchen	Bedroom	Bathroom	Alarm active?	Comment
24 00 to 07 29	off	off	off	off	yes	night time
07 30	off	off	on	off	no	wake up
07 32	off	off	on	on	no	visit bathroom
07 35	off	on	on	off	no	make cup of tea
etc.						

Table 5.1 House lighting requirements

If the user is to enter data, the word **validation** should spring to mind. What checks can be made to see if the data is valid? Times are being entered, so if the 24 hour system is used, then you can make sure that no value exceeds 24 00 or that no value is less than 00 01. Also, check that data such as 13 87 is not entered. (What's wrong with it and what would you do about it?)

If data is to be changed what will the user see on the screen? What messages will be used? This is, effectively, designing the **data capture** form. (Except that, obviously, it will appear on the screen.)

What are you going to call the variables that will be used to represent the various states of the system? Don't forget to use meaningful variable names. A list of what each variable does should appear in your project with the program listing. Some typical names might be as follows.

Variable name	Purpose
alarm$	shows if the alarm is on or off (e.g. alarm$ = 'off.)
bed$	contains the status of the bedroom light (e.g. bed$ = 'on' means that the light in the main bedroom is on)
second$	shows current seconds between 0 and 59
hour$	shows current hours between 0 and 24
etc.	

There will be many variables in the final program. It would be best to introduce them as and when they are needed in the procedures you are going to write. They are mentioned here simply because many variables will have to be **initialized** (set up) at the start of the program.

Compare the progress so far with what you have written in your diary.

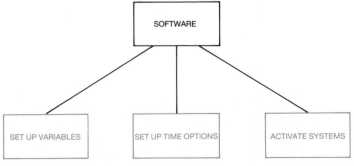

Fig. 5.2 Structure diagram for software

You are now in a position to sort out some of the sub-problems that come under the 'Software' box in Figure 5.1(b). For example, some might be

- set up variables
- set up time
- give user option of changing the data
- activate the system etc.

A new structure diagram for 'Software' can now start to be developed as shown in Figure 5.2.

Progress so far

Much work has now gone into thinking about the system. It is worth mentioning exactly what has been done so far.

(a) A good idea had to be thought up.

(b) The detailed specification had to be produced.

(c) Some limitations of the system were mentioned.

(d) The systems to be used have been thought of.

(e) Your choice of hardware and software must be justified.

(f) The inputs and outputs have been defined.

(g) A structure diagram of the project showing its sub-sections has been drawn up.

(h) Parts of the structure diagram in **(g)** have been considered in more detail and broken down into sub-problems.

(i) Special problems such as 'making a video' and 'building a dolls house' have been identified.

Putting it together

Making a schedule and keeping a diary

The progress so far can be thought of as the **design and analysis phase**. Note that you still have not written a single line of computer program! Instead, you have done the job of a **systems analyst**. The problem has been well thought out, and your method of tackling it has been decided. You may even wish to draw up a simple timetable. You will know the date that your project must be finished (usually in April or early May). By this time you must have written and tested all your hardware and software, taken your photographs or made your video and written all your documentation.

It cannot be stressed strongly enough that you should start to **work hard as early as possible**, and not leave it all to the last minute. With the introduction of the GCSE courses you may well have several projects for different subjects to complete during the same few weeks. There have been students in the past who did not manage to get to bed the night before their final project documentation had to be handed in! Even if you only have your computer studies project to do, you could well find that the computer room is packed with people all trying to get their projects finished.

Documentation is considered in Section Six, but it is worth keeping a diary of all the work you do. In this diary you should write down reasons for any major decisions that you have taken.

An important entry in the diary

As an example, imagine that you are working on the 'house' problem. Suppose that someone said to you, 'What happens if you come home late at 1.00 in the morning and want to get in?' You realize that when you open the front door the alarm will go off.

This is a classic case of not having thought about the specification clearly enough in the first place. However, it must be said that even with the best of specifications, a better way of doing something will come along. You would be perfect if it did not! If the problem *can* be overcome then you should make the modifications needed, and say *why* you are doing them.

In this case, a simple 20 second time delay could allow you enough time to open the door and press a secret button. The alarm would not then sound. Enter this in your diary.

What else?

It is at this stage that the Northern Examining Association require that the design and analysis half of your project be marked. It must therefore be written up in a suitable form. (Don't forget to look at the marking scheme if possible.) It would not be a bad idea to make a rough write-up of what you have done so far even if you *don't* have to. It will help make clear in your mind what you are doing and also be useful later when the proper write-up has to be done. Why not write up some of the project as you go along? Remember that any text that you type into the word processor can be saved and used at a later date.

At last, the computer

Having split the problem up into sub-sections, we can now write *and test* each sub-section. As an example, consider the problem of setting the correct time for the computer-controlled clock in our burglar alarm.

The procedure to set up time

For this problem, assume you are using a BBC computer as described in Section Four (p. 26). The computer has a function called **TIME** that works in **centiseconds** (hundredths of a second). TIME can easily be set to zero at the start of a program by using:

   TIME = 0

Seconds, minutes and hours can be built up by making use of TIME and the MOD and DIV commands in the following way.

seconds = (TIME DIV 100) MOD 60
minutes = (TIME DIV 6000) MOD 60
and   hours = (TIME DIV 360000) MOD 24

(Look in your computer handbook if you don't know about MOD and DIV.)

Seconds, minutes and hours are now variables that can be used elsewhere in the program.

Instead of starting off with TIME = 0, it would be more convenient to set it to the actual time from a digital watch or Ceefax. This could be done by getting the user to type in the hours, minutes and seconds for a particular time, and then pressing a key when that exact time arrives. The following BASIC procedure will perform these operations.

```
10000  DEF PROCset_up_time
10010    INPUT"Initial seconds";initial_seconds
10020    INPUT"Initial minutes";initial_minutes
10030    INPUT"Initial hours";initial_hours
10040    INPUT"PRESS RETURN AT EXACT TIME";dummy$
10050    TIME = ((initial_hours*60 + initial_minutes)*60 + initial_
                                                        seconds)*100
10060  ENDPROC
```

It is always a good idea to have a list of variables and what they do. This is shown in Table 5.2.

Variable name	Type	Purpose
initial_seconds	numeric	sets initial seconds in start up time
initial_minutes	numeric	sets initial minutes in start up time
initial_hours	numeric	sets initial hours in start up time
dummy$	string	serves no purpose other than to delay the program until the exact moment when the user presses the RETURN key
TIME	numeric	a function that counts in centiseconds

Table 5.2 Variables used

Testing the procedure

It is no good going any further *until* the above procedure is fully tested and working. One way of doing this is to write a **testing** procedure which displays the time on the screen. This is shown as follows.

```
20010  DEF PROCtest_time
20020    REPEAT
20030      seconds = (TIME DIV 100) MOD 60
20040      PRINT TAB(26,11);seconds;"   "
20050      minutes = (TIME DIV 6000) MOD 60
20060      PRINT TAB(16,11);minutes;"   "
20070      hours = (TIME DIV 360000) MOD 24
20080      PRINT TAB(7,11);hours;"   "
20090    UNTIL FALSE
20100  ENDPROC
```

Always develop and test your programs in small chunks.

Another point to note is that when the procedures have been written, all that is necessary is to write the main module.

```
10  REM Test and display time routines.
20    PROCset_up_time
20    CLS : REM Clear the screen.
40    PROCtest_time
50  END
```

The procedures shown above would obviously have to be added to this program. In this sort of way the entire project can be developed. i.e. writing a procedure, testing it, then adding it to others that have already been tested.

Keep your program sections fairly short – never with more than 20 to 30 lines. All your sections must be tested in some way, even if this means running part of a procedure.

In the final documentation, cut down your explanation so that all of the documentation (excluding the listings) can be fitted into about 10–20 sides of A4. If necessary, include some **appendices** at the back to cover any additional detail that you feel might be needed.

The control project problems

Whenever a control project is being done there will always be extra information that needs to be put into your report. We consider this special information now.

The circuit diagram

If your project involves wiring some light bulbs or motors etc then you should show exactly how this is done. An example for the computer-controlled burglar alarm is shown in Figure 5.3.

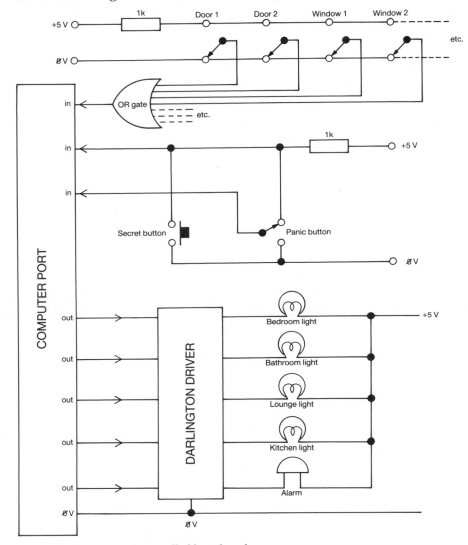

Fig. 5.3 A computer-controlled burglar alarm

If you are not familiar with how circuits should be wired you should get them checked by your teacher. It is especially important to check that they are safe and won't damage the computer to which they are connected.

Never try to connect wires to your computer without checking that the voltages are correct. Also, proper plugs *must* be used so that the wires don't touch each other and damage the system. If you have a proper interface unit at school then *use it*, even if this unit will not appear in the final project.

In some schools, boxes have been built up that enable students to connect wires to the computer easily. Little red and green lights can be used to show if the outputs are 5 V (on) or 0 V (off). If you have not got these units in your computer department then you might be able to borrow one from physics or CDT. If not, you could try persuading your teacher to buy or make one!

The real project You will not be installing this project in an actual house. For the purposes of GCSE you can build a small model and control 5 V bulbs. As a final note you could show how the project is intended to control the real house at a later date. This is shown in Figure 5.4.

A qualified electrician would need to do this wiring

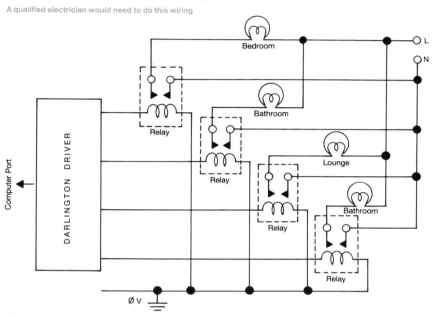

Fig. 5.4 Controlling a real house

Don't forget that, **for safety purposes**, a qualified electrician should carry out the work.

Summary

1 Make sure you have produced the project specification.

2 Mention any limitations that your system will have.

3 Mention the hardware and software that you have at your disposal to solve the problem.

4 Explain why you have made your choices.

5 Realize the extra problems that you may have with control projects:
(a) building hardware
(b) taking photographs, making a video or audio recording.

6 Split the project up into smaller sections. Make use of structure diagrams.

7 Take each sub-section from **(6)** and split them further until the problems are more manageable.

8 Identify:
(a) inputs to the system **(b)** outputs from the system.

9 Design the data capture methods for the input. Don't forget to verify and validate if possible.

10 If you are writing software:
(a) split up the problems into sub-problems using a structure diagram
(b) split each sub-problem up further until you can cope with a single simple problem.

11 Take each simple problem and code it. You must remember to:
(a) specify exactly in words what you are trying to do

(b) write down what each variable in the procedure will do

(c) code no more than about 20 to 30 lines at a single time

(d) use structured programming methods and don't use GOTOs if possible.

12 Test each procedure before going onto any other. Write extra test programs if necessary.

13 Don't add procedures to the main program until they are fully tested.

14 You may need to develop suitable test data. (i.e. unusual combinations of input to the computer).

15 If you are doing a control project, then the details of your computer's port must be given.

16 Any extra circuit diagrams showing how the devices are connected to the computer must be shown.

17 Don't forget to show the system working on the photo or video. It is the project that the moderator wants to see, not pictures of you sitting by the side of the computer!

The newspaper project

The new project

You are the secretary of the school model railway club which produces a club magazine four times a year. The magazine has, in the past, been produced by hand. The text was typed on a typewriter and pictures were either pencil drawings or photographs. The master sheets were photocopied to produce the magazine.

Having briefly seen word processing packages, art packages and desk top publishing packages during your computer studies lessons, you decide to see if the magazine could be produced more professionally using computers. You feel that this problem would be ideal for your GCSE computer studies project.

General background information

The present manual system

There are six pupils who work on the magazine. They are:

- the editor (yourself)
- the feature writer
- the secretary
- the photographer
- the printer
- the artist

Each magazine has one major feature. The feature writer gives the final script to the editor who incorporates it with the other articles, drawings and photographs that have been collected. With the help of the secretary the magazine is typed and a layout is produced. Finally, the printer produces 50 copies of the magazine which go out to the members. You are the only member of the team who understands about computers, so one of your tasks will be to convince the other, non-technical members of the editorial team that using computers may be a better way to produce the magazine. Don't forget that using a computer might *not* be a better way of producing the magazine! You will have to play the role of a **systems analyst**.

The computer-
produced
magazine

Specification

(a) A multi-page magazine consisting of text and pictures is to be produced for the school model railway club.

(b) Text should be produced in a form that can be **imported** into the desk top publishing system and easily edited.

(c) There should be a variety of styles of text.

(d) Checks such as grammar and spelling should be made on the text.

(e) Copies of the magazine should be archived for safe keeping and be easily traceable.

(f) The system should be able to reproduce photographs to a standard at least as good as on the current photocopier.

(g) The system should be able to be used by non-technical people.

Limitations of the system

(a) No laser printer is available and therefore NLQ-type output from a dot matrix printer will be the best available.

(b) The graphics resolution will be limited by the video digitizer and the software and hardware that the computer department has.

(c) No colour printer is available so output will be limited to black and white (as with the present manual system).

(d) There may be many minor limitations imposed by the system. For example, it may be that the printers can't produce the required number of characters per line, or the required number of lines per page etc.

The format of the magazine may well have to change and fit in with what the equipment and software can offer. One of the investigations will be to see if all the advantages outweigh these disadvantages. More expensive systems may obviously overcome these limitations, but costs (they could be well in excess of £5000) would prevent you from having access to them.

> *Make sure you have given enough background information to enable people to understand your project.*

The systems you will use

The school has BBC microcomputers with the following word processors:
- Acornsoft View
- Computer Concepts Wordwise Plus.

The desk top publishing facilities available are:
- AMX Stop Press (formerly called AMX Pagemaker).

The ART package available is:
- AMX Superart.

The printers available are:
- Epson MX80
- Epson FX80
- Brother dot matrix
- Brother daisy wheel.

The digitizer available is:
- Watford Electronics digitizer.

The school also has many utilities such as a spelling checker, and several disc libraries from which pre-digitized pictures such as cars and animals etc can be obtained.

<table>
<tr><td>

How do we start?

</td><td>

As with the other projects, it is best to split up the main problems into more manageable sub-problems. For example, a list of problems (not in any special order) may be:

</td></tr>
</table>

- getting data into the computer system
- getting data from the computer
- the editing process
- the documentation.

Now look at them in detail.

Getting data into the computer system (inputs)

This could be split up as:
- **text information** to be typed into the computer
- **pictures** in the form of **photographs**
- **live pictures** (e.g. a picture of one of the pupils, direct from the video digitizer)
- **diagrams** and **freehand drawings**
- **articles** from other magazines (e.g. text already in typewritten form)
- **logos** and **standard pictures**.

Getting data from the computer

This could be split up into:
- **printing text**
  (a) *different fonts* (styles of text)
  (b) *different sizes*
  (c) *different angles* (e.g. up and down the page.)
- **printing pictures**
- **printing diagrams** (e.g. line drawings)
- **printing digitized pictures**.

The editing processes

These could be split up into sections such as:
- **cutting** and **pasting**
- **printing** rough drafts
- **previewing** on screen.

The documentation

This would be a major section as you would have to write a user's manual for your non-technical members.

Conclusions

From the above processes we should be able to produce a **structure diagram** for the project, part of which is shown in Figure 6.1.

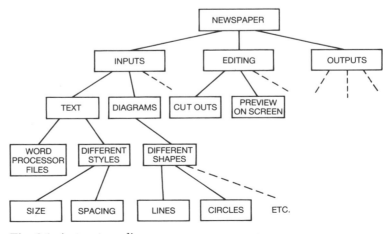

Fig. 6.1 A structure diagram

By now you should have a good idea of what needs to be done but you may also be worried that this sort of project does not fit exactly into some of the examination boards' marking schemes. You may think that it's not like many of the other projects! For example, how can you:

- test input by using **verification** and **validation** techniques
- make sure you have chosen the best methods when so few options are available
- develop suitable test data for the system
- show the development of the system etc?

More students are now using applications packages to solve practical problems and many boards' marking schemes are becoming more flexible. By talking to your teacher, you should be able to find ways of overcoming most problems.

Data capture methods . . . text

If it is possible to validate some of the data say so.

It would be ideal if each member who gave articles to the magazine could present them as a word processor file or on a floppy disc. This is probably unrealistic and so the usual paper scripts will have to be acceptable! This means that there will have to be sessions when the secretary produces the necessary text files. Each text file will have to have a special name which is relevant to the text.

The problems of archiving in the manual system are overcome by having a separate folder for each magazine. When the newspaper files are on computer disc, they can be archived by making use of the hierarchical directory structure available on the BBC Master series or on the ECONET system. The directory structure could be as shown in Figure 6.2.

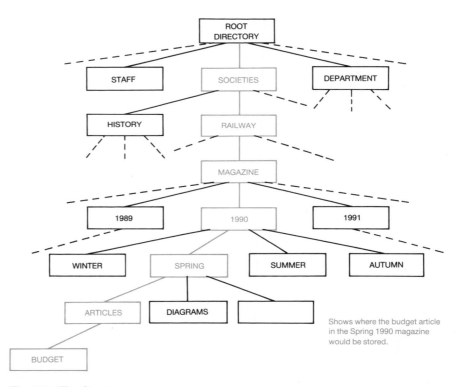

Shows where the budget article in the Spring 1990 magazine would be stored.

Fig. 6.2 The directory structure

Each level in the diagram is a separate directory on the disc. For example, RAILWAY.MAGAZINE.JUNE89.FEATURE would be the **file name** of the main feature for the June '89 edition of the railway club magazine.

Some members of the team would like to have a catalogue that also gave the nature of the articles held on disc. Perhaps this could be the subject of another computer studies project using a database?

Data verification

It *would* be possible for a second person to type in identical text to the first person but under a different file name. You could then make use of a verification utility which checks if two files are identical. However, even very minor differences in typing, such as extra spaces, will appear to be errors. Because of this it will probably be easier to proof read the text manually.

Data validation

Apart from the date and title of the magazine, validation is not possible as the articles are of a random nature. The editor will in any case read the articles and reject any obvious nonsense!

Spelling checks

Each article will be passed through a spelling checker program before being put into a form suitable for the desk top publishing package.

Which word processor?

Any word processor program that produces standard ASCII text will do (this includes most word processors). The disc will have to be in a form that can be read by the BBC computer. The desk top publishing package can import text from both of the school's word processors, so either is acceptable. The ability of the word processors to lay out the text is largely irrelevant as this is done from within the desk top publishing system.

Data capture . . . pictures

There are two main types of picture: **photographs** and **drawings**. Photographs can be digitized and fed directly into the desk top publishing package. Line diagrams can be produced in two ways: either by using the facilities from within the desk top publishing package or by using an art package. The art package is better for more artistic drawings. Technical-type drawings can be done on both systems.

Members of the team will need to spend time using the packages to produce the pictures. The ideal solution would be to get contributors to present their artwork on discs or network files.

Standard pictures can be got from the library and any which are not available can be created or can be digitized from a photograph.

The main project

The first, and perhaps most obvious thing that you will have to do is learn about the systems. This will be time consuming but must be done. If you do not do this, you will not appear to be very expert when you have your first meeting with the other members of the production team.

One option is to produce samples of different text and graphics that can be produced on the system. These can be used as examples of what can be done. Then you can arrange some meetings with the production team. During these meetings you can arrange for a demonstration of the word

processors, art packages and desk top publishing systems. You are taking the role of a **systems analyst** trying to convince people that the system you are demonstrating could be right for their needs and better than the existing manual system.

The demonstration lectures

(*Three 40 minute sessions*)
These lectures will be given to the other five members of your team. The purpose is *not* to teach anybody how to operate the systems, but to show how things can easily be done using the systems.

(a) Simple demonstration of the word processor

Show the following:
- text entry
- simple editing
- saving text on disc with appropriate file names
- loading text from disc
- more advanced editing and formatting

(b) Demonstration of the art package

1 Introduce the mouse and icons.
2 Draw simple shapes.
3 Demonstrate spray, line and fill modes.
4 Show how to edit the picture using a rubber.
5 Show how to edit each pixel with the zoom facility.
6 Create a simple picture and save on disc.
7 Do a screen dump to the printer.

(c) Demonstration of the desk top publishing package

1 Show how to enter text.
2 Show different font styles. Note that, just because there are 25 styles available you don't have to use them all on one page. Have magazines available to see how the professionals do it.
3 Show how to arrange text in windows.
4 Show how to move text on the page.
5 Show simple drawing facilities.
6 Create a simple picture.
7 Show facilities such as 'rotate' etc.
8 Do a screen dump.

Don't forget that it is your responsibility to convince your teachers and the moderator that you have done this. You could make a small presentation folder of your lecture notes and handouts (e.g. the screen dumps of the different types of text etc). Perhaps you can include one or two overhead projector transparencies to convince them that it really happened.

The magazine

After convincing the board with your three lectures, you will need to start on your **trial production run**. You will use the computer to produce the magazine and then compare it with the *same* magazine produced by the *old* methods.

You decide to use the following criteria to check if the exercise has been successful.
- time to produce the master copy
- convenience
- versatility
- professional appearance
- reliability
- ease of use.

One of the main problems will be with the first item above – the time involved! This is because *you* are the only person who understands how to use the system. It would be unfair to take account of time spent learning how to use the computers. Therefore, you have decided to do all the jobs yourself. This is not unreasonable as it is *your* computer studies project. The other members of the team will continue with the manual method, but watch how you progress.

The new logo

To launch the new-style 'Train of Thought' (the magazine's name!) you decide to create a new logo. The team decides that it would be nice to have an old steam train with the title of the magazine somehow written on top of the train. The logo must not take up more than one quarter of the front page, and should include space for the date and edition within the logo.

Producing the logo . . . the processing

Possible methods of production could be:

- drawing the train dot by dot
- producing a digitized image from a photograph
- looking in the transport utilities library.

The first method is tedious in the extreme. You have to be a good artist to produce acceptable results. Even then, it takes a long time.

The third method is easy. However, this assumes that a suitable picture exists.

If no picture exists then a suitable photograph will have to be found and digitized.

Solution

Fortunately, a suitable size and shape photograph appear in the System Mnemonics Cut-out Library. A draft screen dump of the locomotive is shown in Figure 6.3.

> *Record all the important trial and error sessions in your diary.*

Fig. 6.3 The locomotive

The cut-out can be loaded into the desk top publishing system and positioned ready for the addition of the title. You will need to set up a window in the design of the engine for the text, but due to the black background, an appropriate style of text with a white outline must be used to produce a white background in which the text can be seen.

Experiments with different text sizes and fonts will have to be carried out and the best results printed out for selection.

The system is very versatile because you can preview on the screen what

Fig. 6.4 The finished logo

the final result will look like. If you don't like the chosen font, you can wipe the window and start again without destroying the picture of the loco. The final result is shown in Figure 6.4.

The main articles and feature

There are no problems with the typing of the text into the word processors. The format of the text is unimportant. The layout will be taken care of by using windows when the text is read into the desk top publishing system. Before the text leaves the word processors it should be proof read and automatically checked for spelling mistakes.

Checking for spellings

Text from either word processor can be checked for spelling mistakes. This is done by using the spelling checker program. It compares the text word for word with a dictionary held on another disc. Any words not in the dictionary are brought to the attention of the user and corrected if necessary. The user also has the option of adding the word to the dictionary if it is correct, so that the computer will recognize it next time. Names of all the members of the club and special railway technical terms such as *fishplate* and *sleepers* can also be added.

The archives . . . text

Two separate floppy discs for each magazine edition will be needed to back up all text. Appropriate file names will also need to be chosen. These back-up discs must then be stored in separate rooms in case of accident or fire.

The other artwork

The **artwork** for the magazine consists of photographs which have to be digitized, art-type drawings such as cartoons, and technical-type line drawings.

Photographs

Make sure that you demonstrate that any validation and verification has been carried out.

Having digitized a photograph and produced a screen dump, you may well feel that the finished product is of too poor quality to be useful. The original photographs can be photocopied quite well, to produce a much better quality image for the master copy. You therefore decide not to use the digitizer for this process. Don't forget that this is the sort of important entry that should be put in your diary. This makes the final results and conclusions much easier to present.

The video digitizer

You can use a video digitizer with a video camera or video recorder to capture a still image. This image is already in the same form on disc as the other library utilities mentioned earlier. The advantage of the digitizer is that it enables you to take a picture of a member of the club without the need for photographic processing. The quality is not very good with the current (8-bit) generation of computers and desk top publishing packages. When the true 32-bit machines become widespread, however, the quality will be excellent, especially if you have a laser printer.

Where the digitizer does come into its own is in its ability to produce a real image which can then be altered. For example, you might do an article on what you think the editorial team will be doing in 20 years time. You could digitize the image of the editor and then, once it is in digital form, you could spray a beard onto his face and make him look 20 years older!

Cartoon diagrams

These can be produced on the AMX superart package. Figure 6.5 shows a typical example.

Fig. 6.5 A typical cartoon

It is generally easier to use a pencil and paper than to draw the cartoon with a mouse. Even so, once the original image has been created it can be altered more easily using the art package. The original line work for the cartoon could be digitized and fed into the computer. The colouring in can then be done in the art package. This assumes that your school does not possess a graphics tablet, which is a device that enables you to draw using a pencil. The results then appear on the screen.

Technical drawings

Both the art package and desk top publishing package are good at producing simple technical-type drawings. Examples are shown in Figure 6.6.

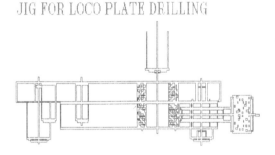

Fig. 6.6 Technical drawings

The archives . . . drawings

Due to the nature of the system, all diagrams will be saved on a disc that is formated in a special way. This means that diagrams can't be saved on the same disc as the text files. Again, two separate floppy discs will be needed for each magazine. So, with the text discs, four floppy discs are needed altogether for each magazine. The system is therefore more expensive than the manual folders method.

Doing the editing

Mention any advantages/ disadvantages your system may have compared to the manual methods.

After all the features, articles and artwork have been assembled the next stage is to decide how the magazine is to be laid out.

Manual methods

At present this is a major problem. It may be necessary to make many attempts at laying out the text with the typewriter. Many sheets of paper will get torn up and thrown in the bin. The only feasible way is to photocopy the articles and cut them up and paste them onto the master sheet. This is very frustrating and the final result does not always look professional.

Computer-based methods

The method of importing text from word processors depends on the creation of special windows. The idea is shown in Figure 6.7(a).

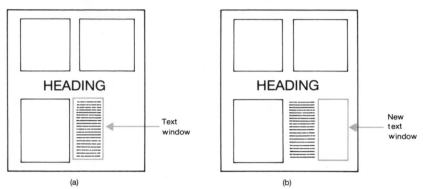

Fig. 6.7 Windows

Fig. 6.8

You set up a window as shown in Figure 6.7(a). Then you import text to the window until it is full. You can then define another window as shown in Figure 6.7(b), and continue with the entry of the text.

In practice, because the text is not formed in the normal way, a grid must be defined. This enables you to line up the text so that the spaces between lines are the same throughout several different windows when joined together.

An advantage of this method is that it is easy to start again if you don't like the layout. Also, a whole window may easily be moved to a different part of the screen if necessary. Windows may be **inverted** (white on a black background for special effects) or have **borders** added to them.

It is still not easy to get the perfect page layout without lots of practice, but it is very much easier and less frustrating than using the manual methods. So, using this method, you are more likely to strive for a professional-looking document each time.

The results

Two pages of the magazine are shown in Figure 6.8 and Figure 6.9. As can be seen from the two-page sample, a reasonably professional-looking

Railway Society Photographic Competition.

This is the issue in which we launch our annual photo competition.
This year the theme is SPEED. We would like you to produce a photo which shows a train at speed.
Anything won't do. Let your special effects genius shine through.
You have got until the end of September to come up with the goods. Entries to the society secretary please. Best of luck. The winning entry will be shown in "Train of Thought". Wow!!

MEGA EVENT
OF THE YEAR.

Yes folks! It's here again.

The Railway Society annual dinner and musical evening will be held in the school canteen on the last Friday of term.
During the evening members and their girlfriends will demonstrate their musical talents by playing the spoons, knives and forks, or any other cutlery that comes to hand! Members may even bring along a musical instrument.

Tickets Two pounds each.

Doors open at 7pm. BE THERE! (Finish 11 p.m.)

Fig. 6.9

magazine has been produced. The only real criticism of it is that it is not possible to create text that is small enough.

Conclusions

When any conclusions are drawn about the work you have done it is important to compare what you have actually achieved with what you set out to achieve. You will remember that on page 47 we set out the criteria by which the systems would be judged. We now look at each of these in turn.

Time to produce the master copy

For the purpose of this project, the time needed to train people to use the system has been discounted. Although it would be an important consideration if the production team decided to go ahead, it was considered unfair to include it at this stage. The actual time needed to produce the magazine was similar to that for the manual system. This is due to the greater degree of experimentation that went on when using the computer system.

Convenience

> *It is most important to say how effective your project has been.*

This depends very much on who you are. For example, producing the text on word processors is much more convenient for the secretary due to the tremendous power of the system to edit the text and check spellings etc. Hard copy of each article must be produced, though, as otherwise, any editorial meetings would have to be held in front of the computer, which is not so convenient!

Back-up copies of discs need to be made and stored in a safe place. This is all very well in an office but is less convenient in school where people carry their belongings around in bags, and have been known to leave them in playgrounds! The discs cost money, and therefore the magazines are more expensive to produce.

As for artwork, a combination of using packages and photographs seems best. Therefore, the total computerization of the magazine seems impossible at this stage. However, even someone with little artistic ability can produce copy of a quality ready for printing in the magazine.

Versatility

The computer system wins hands down. What can be produced is excellent when compared to the results of the manual system. Even so, there is a price to pay here. No longer can the magazine be produced at home on the old typewriter. In the past this has proved a useful thing to be able to do.

Professional appearance

It is much easier to get a good looking magazine with the computerized system. As the equipment gets more sophisticated, the results will be even better.

Reliability

The system is very reliable as long as nobody presses any wrong buttons by mistake! This is all very well for the trained person but can be frustrating for someone new to computers. The **user's guide**, which comes in the documentation system, should help overcome most of the problems.

Ease of use

The system is very easy to use once it has been understood. It would be hard for a person new to computing to learn all the systems at once. Therefore, if the system is introduced, a training program would have to be set up. This is a lot of work. Do the results justify it?

Checklist

1 Have you specified the present manual methods used and said who will be using the system?

2 Have you drawn up a specification for the system and included any limitations of your system?

3 Have you specified the exact hardware and software packages that you will use?

4 Have you split up the problem to be solved into **inputs**, **outputs** and **processing**?

5 Have you covered **verification** and **validation**? Also, what happens if a disc is corrupted or lost?

6 Have you described what systems are available and *justified* why you are doing things in a particular way?

7 Have you developed enough information to show how your problems are going to be solved? The above is developing your method of solution (i.e. the **algorithm**).

8 Have you produced enough material to convince the moderator that your solution works?

9 If there are unforeseen problems during the development of your system then put them in your diary. Mention them under the implementations section of your project.

10 Have you made any comparisons between the old manual methods you are trying to replace and the new computerized systems you are developing?

11 Have you tested the system to make sure that it does all that you wanted it to? If so, what do the results look like? Is there any test data that you can develop? Does it cover all possibilities?

12 When considering any conclusions to your project you must be critical. It is unlikely to be perfect and you can gain marks by saying how it could be improved if you were to start again.

Shall we or shan't we?

Everybody agreed that the final results justified the computerization of the magazine. Learning the new systems was fun, but was going to take up a large amount of time initially. One of the spin-offs is that more people could become involved in the production of the magazine, producing copy almost in its final state. There will still be the scraps of paper handed in, but these can be easily dealt with.

The documentation

When the documentation for this project is written there will have to be a large specialized section in the user manual explaining the roles of each person in the production team. The idea is not to replace the manuals for each of the systems; that would be impossible. The aim is to guide people – for example, the artist needs help with the computer process of producing pictures.

Section Eight is about how to write different types of documentation. We have therefore not included any in this section.

As with the other projects in this book, this section only represents highlights of what a good project should contain. Much more technical details of the packages being used would be required for a project of this type.

Summary

1 Make sure that you have produced a suitable specification.

2 Mention any limitations that your system will have.

3 Make sure that you have covered the hardware and software that you intend to use.

4 Justify any choices that you have made.

5 Split up the problem to be solved into more manageable parts.

6 Draw systems diagrams to show the overall plan of your solution.

7 Make sure that you have covered:
- data validation
- data verification
- what to do if the power fails etc.

8 Identify any of your project's special problems; e.g. the project in this section needed you to produce three lectures with handouts for your 'pupils'.

9 Experiment with various ways of solving your sub-problems.

10 Give some examples of your best solutions.

11 Write down in your diary any problems that you encounter.

12 Produce a suitable solution for your project, i.e. the result.

13 Make a critical analysis of what you have done.

14 Say how things could have been done better.

Some project ideas

If you have read the first sections of this book you should by now have a very good idea about how to tackle a project. What is not so easy is choosing one in the first place! In this section are some different suggestions for projects. Only the basic ideas will be discussed here, the rest is up to you.

Consult your teacher first

Many schools now have excellent computer equipment and some of the following ideas are based on equipment that has been placed into schools under various government schemes. Some of these items of equipment may not be in the computer department, but other members of staff are usually helpful if you wish to do a project using their equipment, especially if they could use the software afterwards. However, do check with your teachers to see whether the equipment *is* available and *can* be used.

An interactive video system

Interactive video systems can be found in some schools. They are proving more popular and will certainly present many project ideas in the future. An interactive video system (or IVS for short) is a computer system which controls a **laser player**. A laser player is similar in principle to a video player (the playback system of a video recorder), but instead of using video tape, it makes use of a disc called a **laser disc**. You could imagine it to be rather like an overgrown compact disc, but *video* as well as *audio* information is carried on the disc. One such system made up from a Research Machines Nimbus PC computer, a Sony video disc player and an interactive video system by Next Technology Ltd is shown in Figure 7.1.

Fig. 7.1 The IVS system at Tonbridge School

The possibilities for projects are many and varied. You have complete control over the player, right down to the ability to display a single frame of video information (i.e. a still picture). The quality is also superb. The computer allows you to superimpose text and graphics on the screen. This means that you can display text, graphics, sound and video information all at the same time! It really does give you the power of a film editor.

How is it done?

It may sound very complicated, but in practice it could not be simpler. Imagine, for the sake of argument, that the video disc has 100 000 frames of video information on it. If you want to display frame number 7000 then a command like:

STILL 7000

is all you need. This can easily be written as a simple single line command in a BASIC program.

If you want to run a sequence of frames in real time then:

PLAY 5000, 5300

might be all that is necessary to run the video from frame 5000 until frame 5300. The response is almost instantaneous because there is no video tape to rewind. It is like a compact disc. The head can be moved directly to the right part of the disc and the disc rotates so that the correct frame of information is located within a fraction of a second.

If you want to play the video backwards in slow motion then:

STEP 10, 2 REV

might be the command to step back through 10 frames with a 2 second delay between frames.

AUDIO ON and AUDIO OFF

might be the commands to turn the sound on and off. It really is *that easy* to control an interactive video system.

Don't limit your project to equipment found only in the computer department.

Combining text, graphics, video and sound

The possibilities are endless. Imagine that you have a video about volcanoes, showing some spectacular eruptions. Really colourful shots will maintain the interest of most audiences. Now suppose that you wish to show a bar chart indicating the areas of the world in which most volcanic eruptions take place. Imagine using the background of an erupting volcano to add dynamic interest to the video display. If you choose your colours for the bar chart correctly they can easily stand out from the background.

This type of system can become an electronic book. Text can be displayed on screen and can be followed by a related video display rather like looking at an illustration in a book. The change to video would be controlled by the user. It's exactly like reading a page of a book, then looking at the picture on the next page. The only difference here is that the picture actually comes to life in full colour with sound.

The availability of the discs

At the time of writing this book it must be said that not many video discs are available (perhaps 10 or 20). Therefore, unless you are lucky enough to be able to make your own video (a time-consuming and costly business) then your choice of material will be limited to the contents of the recorded video images. However, if your school has got an IVS system, then opportunities exist for some really exciting projects to be done.

A MIDI music system

A few years ago MIDI had not been developed. Today it is the **standard** for connecting musical instruments to a computer. Indeed today most micros either have a MIDI port or one can be connected using an interface.

MIDI stands for **Musical Instrument Digital Interface**. It is used mainly for the computer control of keyboards, synthesizers and drum machines, although more instruments are being added.

Figure 7.2 shows a Korg Poly 800 synth keyboard connected to an Archimedes computer running the studio 24 software from EMR.

Projects with MIDI, like most other projects and other software packages, can be tackled on different levels. Perhaps the most obvious ones for MIDI software would be:

● writing your own software to control the MIDI hardware directly

● making use of prewritten packages that enable you to build up files of music and edit them to produce special effects etc

● adding special features to some previously developed MIDI package.

Fig. 7.2 A MIDI set up
at Tonbridge School

MIDI project type 1

The first type of project as listed above is not for the faint-hearted. You would have to understand how the MIDI system controls the instrument at a very technical level. This would be comparable to writing an assembly language program, and is therefore not recommended for the majority of students.

MIDI project type 2

The second level is similar to using a package such as a database. You would define what type of musical scores and effects you wanted. Then you would have to set up the system to achieve exactly what you had in mind. This would involve building up files of music and editing them until the results were exactly what you wanted.

The main output from the above system would – hopefully – be the melodious music coming from the synthesizer! Even so, it would be unusual if this were not accompanied by the musical score printed out, the data necessary to achieve the result and other special files. For example, you may have a separate file for each musical instrument and other files defining the timing of the system etc.

Even some of the simple systems are quite sophisticated. You can record tracks from actual instruments and digitize them. More easily, you can play directly into the MIDI keyboard (as opposed to the computer keyboard) and get the computer to capture your tracks via the MIDI interface. You can then replay the tracks and add a different track while the computer is replaying the original one. In this way one person can build up an entire orchestra of sounds. Professional musicians often use this method when they are developing albums by themselves. However, their equipment would be very much better than that which is found in most schools.

One of the biggest advantages with the synth and MIDI computer control is that if you get a few notes wrong then you can recall the score on the computer and edit the notes. There are few students who don't enjoy

playing back their creations over the power amplifiers at maximum volume!

Be careful that you don't get too carried away making music. You are, after all, carrying out a *computer studies project!* You must concentrate on the data, files, formats, results and technical details to enable you to write up your project report effectively.

Some people may think that this is not a suitable computer studies project. There is no reason why it shouldn't be, if it is conducted in a structured way under supervision. After all, you are allowed to use a word processor as a subject of study for your project. Instead of processing letters that make up text, you are processing notes that make up music. The word processor is a very convenient way of producing and editing text. The MIDI system is an equally convenient way of making and editing music.

MIDI project type 3

This would probably be a 'modifying existing software' type project as stated in Section Two of this book. The ideas for this type of project would involve programming in a high level language such as BASIC. What you can do is limited only by your imagination. Consider the following example.

Many wonderful new ideas end up as ordinary basic programs.

Suppose that you already have a MIDI system that lets you control the MIDI port directly from BASIC. It may be that the notation used is totally user unfriendly. For example:

        PLAY 100,3,8

might be the syntax needed to play note number 100 for three seconds using voice number 8. (The voice is a different sound.) You can imagine trying to compose your heavy metal symphony using masses of statements like the one above!

You could develop and design a system which accepts input in a much more user friendly form. For example, your system could automatically change the commands into a sequence of statements such as that shown above, which would then control the MIDI port. The form of your more user friendly notation would be up to you, but it might involve entering the notes on a musical stave, or else entering the notes using their musical names.

Suppose that you considered the musical stave method mentioned above. Your project would then end up as a BASIC graphical programming exercise. The only thing to do with MIDI would be the codes needed to operate the musical instrument. Such a project would be ideal for computer studies, but you would have to have lots of patience while developing the graphics.

You will be surprised how many students start off on weird and wonderful projects only to find that they are back in the land of BASIC computer programming! This shows the power of the computer. Once you have defined your problem well enough you can often solve it by using software packages or writing your own programs.

Don't forget your hard-worked teachers

If you chose a project such as MIDI, then you should not expect your teachers to be instant experts, able to solve all the problems that you are likely to come up against. Indeed if your teachers are brave enough to let you use projects such as MIDI controllers then be patient while they try and help you. It is probably new to them as well.

A computer aided design package

Think of a good use for your CAD system. Don't just draw a picture.

As with most other projects it is useful to find someone with a specific need, or even design something sensible for yourself. With a good CAD package the possibilities are enormous.

The CAD systems will enable people with an interest in engineering, architecture and related subjects to use a computer to produce designs for systems which are really exciting.

It depends how much CAD you have learnt in your course, but you would be well advised to find out more about it by going round local industry and offices to see how sophisticated systems are used there, then you will come back to school full of ideas. You can then undertake some simpler project on the computers at school, assuming that the equipment is available. Figure 7.3 shows Autosketch running on the Archimedes computer.

The sort of things that immediately spring to mind are designing a car or a house. However, you must be very careful that your project does not degenerate into simply drawing pretty pictures. This would be of little use in gaining marks for your project.

A computer-designed dream home

It is always best to have a specific aim in mind. For example, in this energy-conscious time in which we live, why not try to design a house that is very well insulated and therefore inexpensive to heat? It is not really all that difficult.

First you will have to find lots of information about some materials used in the building of new houses. This is easy. You simply write to a builder,

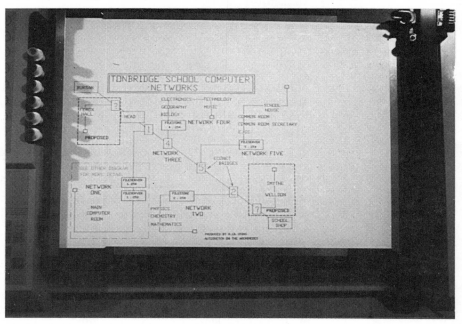

Fig. 7.3 Autosketch running on an ARC at Tonbridge School

an architect or a body like the NHBC. Copies of these letters always look good in an appendix at the back of your project reports! If you can't be bothered to write, then you may find a physics book with the information you require. The information involves **U-values**. The U-value is simply the number of watts per square meter, per degree centigrade, lost through the material. Using these values, the wall areas, window areas, ceiling areas together with the temperature difference between the inside and the outside of this house, you can calculate the amount of heat lost and hence the price to heat the house to a certain temperature.

Having found suitable areas and materials you can start to design your ideal house on the CAD package. With a good package you could aim for a 'see-through' three-dimensional plot of the house, and some two-dimensional views of different parts of the house. Look at some builders' plans if you are not familiar with the symbols used on building plans for houses. In this way you are not simply drawing a picture of a house but designing a house, to a given specification, which is cheap to run. You will also be specifying the materials used in the house. If you have time you could compare different shapes of houses to see the effect on the heating bills.

If your school has a plotter then use this to output your CAD diagrams. It makes a much better impression than a graphics dump on a dot matrix printer.

A spreadsheet could be used to add up all the U-values, areas etc and the data could be extracted by a word processor to be inserted in your final report.

What started off as a simple picture of a house on a computer has now turned into a full-blown, top-rate project making use of multiple software packages. This will convince your teachers that you are a good, all-round computer studies student.

Don't forget to discuss simple ideas with your teachers. They can often be developed, like the one above, into very good project ideas. Don't forget the moral of the story. *Make the project useful*.

An art package

CAD is fine for the technically minded, but what if you prefer art to technical drawing? Art packages have come a long way in the last five years. Long gone are the simple systems that gave you a few gaudy colours and crude shapes to choose from. With the introduction of the 32-bit micros such as the IBM PS/2 and the Acorn Archimedes, packages have been developed specially for these systems which are very good indeed. When such a machine is used with a colour printer the possibilities for creative design are great. Pictures of near photographic quality are possible, sometimes in 4096 colours or more. (In industry there are systems which offer you over a million different shades of colour!) The following project is just one of the many that you could possibly choose. Don't think that you can't do good projects on a small micro – you can.

Fashion fabric design using an art package

When designing patterns for fabrics for clothes it is tedious to have to draw them out by hand, and then use colouring pencils to give an idea of colour. How much more convenient it would be to use the computer to work out these details. You can then concentrate on the creative aspects of the design.

A possible way forward

As with many other projects, you are probably wondering how this could fit into writing up a computer studies report. Computer studies is simply a study of anything that uses a computer; there must be a way!

The process of designing patterns can be broken down into simple stages,

one of which must be the basic pattern
without any colour added – a black
and white pencil sketch of shapes.
These may be triangles, stars or more
likely, very complex, more pleasing
shapes. If you are designing fabric
then, as fabric comes in a long roll, it
is obvious that the pattern must be
repeated over and over again. It must,
therefore, consist of a basic pattern
formed from basic shapes.

A file of these basic shapes could be a starting point for your designs.
These shapes could be stored on disc, called up by the art package and
used to make shapes that are repeated in all directions. This process is a
common one and is ideally suited to computerization.

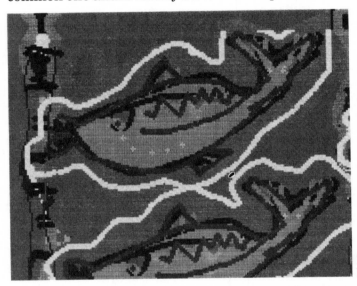

Fig. 7.4 Using a simple
basic shape

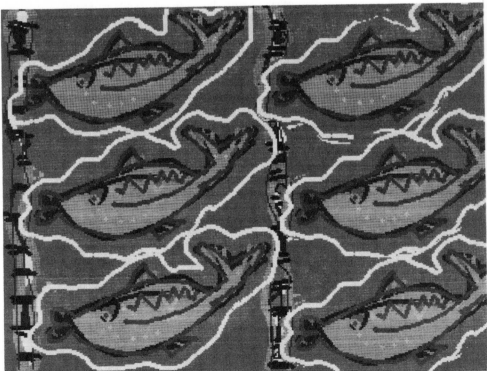

A simple basic shape is shown in Figure 7.4(a) and a pattern made up from this basic shape is shown in Figure 7.4(b). Once the basic pattern has been established you could save this on disc in another file. Don't forget that the original template could be used to make up many basic patterns by overlapping in different ways.

Some art packages will allow you to change the size and relative shape of your basic pattern. You could call up a mirror image of your pattern and reflect it several ways. You could put copies of smaller patterns inside bigger ones. You can rotate a pattern or zoom in and alter a small part of it.

Once pleasing patterns have been established you can load the appropriate files into the art package on the computer for colouring. You should be able to choose an area to colour by filling in an enclosed space. Once the space has been filled it is often possible to change the shade of colour to get the most pleasing effects. You could even add chequered patterns or dots to these enclosed areas.

If you have a suitable plotter, then better effects could be produced on much larger pieces of paper. Why not combine your designs in a fashion show with your friends? You could ask them to give their opinions on your designs and then include the results in your project folder along with your portfolio.

Why not visit a fashion house which specializes in designing fabrics on computer? You will then get many more ideas. You will also see how the computerized patterns are actually turned into practical designs on the fabric.

Why limit the patterns to clothes?

Clothes were used as a good example of an application of the above system. However, wallpaper, Christmas wrapping paper, carpets and many other pattern applications could have been chosen instead.

A viewdata project

Using a network for a viewdata project

It would be unusual if your school did not have some sort of computer network. The two main educational systems have been developed by Acorn and Research machines. Both of these systems give good opportunities for students to develop viewdata systems similar in principle to the Prestel system set up by British Telecom, or the Ceefax, Fourtel and Oracle systems set up by the BBC and ITV television companies. There can be nobody studying computing that has not used or at least seen these systems in operation.

It would be a rare teacher who would let you do a project using a system like Prestel all the time. The phone bills would be astronomic. However, much more fun can be had setting up your own databases using simulations of these systems available on the school networks.

The local viewdata systems

If your school has a computer network, many good projects can be done making use of it.

These are called local viewdata systems because they are used on the local area networks found in schools. The idea is similar to Prestel in that the system contains many pages of information.

One of the most important concepts for projects of this kind is that of **page routing** – the routes you can take in going from one page to another. Usually the system is set up such that each section takes you down a different route until you get to the end. You can then be directed back to the main menu of the system. Indeed you can normally get back to the main menu of the system by pressing a special key at any time.

Setting up a typical system

First you need to decide what information you wish to have present. As with all other projects, make it useful for someone. Imagine that you have had an interview with the headteacher of your school, and together you have decided to set up an experimental bulletin board. If the experiment is successful then some extra hardware may be purchased to have electronic notice boards at various points around the school. It could include the following categories:

- important messages for the day
- school club messages
- sports messages.

The system is only experimental and so these three categories will do to provide a starting point.

The menu system

The main menu will probably consist of a colourful page together with a suitable title and the three categories offered.

Bulletin board

1 Messages for the day
2 School club messages
3 Sports messages

After you have logged onto the system then the main menu should automatically be displayed. You will not have to worry about producing any complex log on procedures as the database will be public. Also, the network manager in your school will probably provide any routing necessary to get your system up and running.

A typical sub menu

As an example, take the sports messages above. You could arrange for the sports page from the main menu to appear when the number 3 is typed. By setting up the system as above, you are then routed onto the main menu for the sports page. Systems such as Commutel on the Econet network allow you to do this with ease. Other systems are just as good.

The sports menu page will probably consist of a suitable title. In addition to these titles it is usual to increase the impact of the system by having suitable graphics as well. This is often done by using a special purpose editor to produce very low resolution coloured graphics of the sort you see on the TV teletext system. They are worth doing as they create a good impression and maintain the user's interest in the system.

The sports page might have the following sub sections.

School sporting menu

1 Football
2 Rugby
3 Hockey
4 Squash
5 Swimming
To return to the main menu press ESC.

By pressing one of the appropriate keys the user will be routed either back to the main menu or onto the chosen sport.

Suppose the user chooses Rugby. The new page, together with a suitable graphic might display:

Rugby fixture list

1 Senior 1st 15
2 Senior 2nds
3 Junior 1st 15
4 Junior 2nds
To return to the sports menu press 9.
To return to the main menu press ESC.

A further press of key 1 might reveal the following:

As always, make your project useful.

The first 15 chosen for this Saturday's match are:

Name	Form	Name	Form
Bishop M.H.	L 6th a	Pendered P.S.	U 6th c
Elliot M.S.	U 6th b	Richards A.N.	L 6th e
Commings P.G.	L 6th c	Rowan M.G.	U 6th b
Duncan M.D.D.	U 6th a	Sanders D.C.	L 6th c
Gales G.P.	L 6th b	Stevens R.J.	U 6th d
Jones K.M.J.	U 6th e	Tebay H.G.	U 6th a
Longley R.I.	U 6th a	Williams G.T.	L 6th c
Lord N.J.	U 6th a		

Reserves:	Jennings S.	U 6th f
	Stead K.J.	U 6th f

To return to the main sports menu press 9.
To return to the main menu press ESC.

You can see from this that you are simply setting up a hierarchical data structure in which the pages form the basic items of information.

A word of warning

Some excellent projects can be done along these lines. However, be warned, make sure that if you manage to set up a successful system, you don't get left with the job of typing in all the data every time it changes. This is a boring, repetitive and tedious task if carried out continually by one person. Ideally, there should be a team of people who take it in turns to manage the database. Perhaps one or two people should be responsible for each section. The information *must* be kept up to date or you will find that the system is eventually useless.

A satellite system

There are two or three systems now on the market which enable schools to receive information directly from satellites. A picture of the **NOAA/METEOSAT** system in use is shown in Figure 7.5. You can see the BBC computer, and associated hardware. You can also see data on the screen obtained from a previous satellite pass.

NOAA and METEOSAT are weather satellite systems. They pass periodically over this country (they are not **geostationary**). Therefore, you might have to be up at the crack of dawn if you want some particular information. However, you *can* set it in **automatic mode**!

Much live data can be obtained automatically when the satellite passes over. This data is in a form that can be simply read and stored on disc. You do not have to be able to understand any electronics or satellite control systems to be able to make use of a project of this nature.

Some of the data sent down will look like gobbledegook. However, you can make sense of it because it is all explained in the manuals which accompany the system. The manuals even show you how to get graphs of the satellites orbit printed out on the dot matrix printer. It's always interesting running the prediction programs which tell you where the satellite is at any particular moment.

If you are thinking of doing a project making use of NOAA or METEOSAT then it would be a good idea to do it in combination with a member of staff from the geography or physics department, who could help you interpret the data. Indeed your project will probably end up as a data capture and analysis project using items of data obtained from the satellite over a long period of time.

You would need to build up a store of data so that it can be analysed at some later time. You could then import the data into some graph-plotting software package and make a nice folder showing the variation of the desired effects over a period of time.

Fig. 7.5 The system running on a BBC computer

As well as NOAA and METEOSAT, it is possible to get **UoSSat** information in a similar form. Information can be printed out on the dot matrix printer and interesting computer projects can result from the analysis of this data. For example, if the physics department were interested in seeing how the Earth's magnetic field varied with time over a period of several months, then this could be done using this system.

You're not still stuck are you?

If you *still* can't think of anything to do or have not got the necessary equipment to do what you would like, there follows a simple list of other possible project titles. They are from many varied and different areas of the curriculum. The ones mentioned in the book are indicated. Some areas in which to beware are also indicated. Don't forget they are only suggestions. Take an idea you like and develop it in a different direction, with your teacher.

Project titles

> *This list is a small sample. Ask your teachers for other ideas.*

Project	Comments
Archive programs	Use the computer to make a catalogue of items that you find interesting, such as old cars. Use cross references to make it interesting.
Artificial intelligence programs	Find out about a program called Eliza.
Art packages	See page 65.
Assembly language projects	**Don't** unless absolutely necessary for part of your project.
Bar code project	Program to produce or read bar codes. Need bar code reader and interface.
Banking	Set up the files for a simple school bank system.

Burglar alarm project	See page 35.
CAD package	See page 64.
CDT programs	A lot of scope for electronics buffs. But see reservations on page 42.
Chemistry programs	See member of staff from the chemistry department for ideas.
CNC project	If your school has any CNC machines in the workshops they may let you do a project using them.
Computer dating agency	Keep it respectable!
Computer studies programs	E.g. logic simulations low level language simulation See teacher for many others.
Data analysis for scientific experiments	E.g. biology field trips geography field trips.
Databases	See Sections Three and Four.
Desk top publishing	See page 45.
Diary planner	
Diet analysis	See page 11.
Digital clock lock	Get the computer to open a door only when the correct codes are typed in. Computer can monitor and log time of entry and people etc.
Disabled persons	There are many projects, all of which are extremely worthwhile for obvious reasons. See local special schools etc.
Dog race predictions	Get the computer to analyse form and print out likely winners! Need plenty of newspapers.
Electronic mail	Can be done on the school network.
Electronics programs	Tempting to build a robot but you won't get many marks for it. However, some good ones can be done. See page 35.
Expert systems	How about building up a very simple medical data base with some question and answer techniques for diagnosis?
Football program	See page 13.
Games programs	**Don't!** (With the possible exception of writing an interactive game for many users on a network. This demonstrates many network capabilities.)
Geography programs	See member of geography department.
Golf tournament scoreboard	Hole by hole analysis of each player and scoreboard shown on screen.
History programs	Mainly analysis of data but your teacher might have a good simulation or other idea.
Household budgeting	See page 74.
Interactive video project	See page 59.
Language programs	Most good programs have already been written. It's easy to do bad projects so beware. However, you may have a brilliant idea!
Library program	Help computerize a small departmental library.

Maths program	Don't! They are usually terrible unless you have an exceptional idea.
MIDI project	See page 61.
Motor vehicle project	Engine simulation but see CDT teacher for others.
Music programs	See page 61.
Payroll program	More difficult to do well than it sounds.
PERT	If your school has a PERT system use it to carry out an analysis of a project.
Physics programs	See physics teacher for ideas.
Poetry	Computers have been used to generate poetry in the past. Not an easy project!
Point of sale program	Type in codes for the tuck in the school shop and generate detailed customer receipts.
Pollution monitoring	Make sure you can get the necessary instruments.
Queuing simulations	Simulating customers arriving at petrol pumps and being served etc. Need random numbers.
Race timing systems	Broken beam starts and stops computer clock. Analysis of several races in files.
Railway project	A computer-controlled train set. Need simple timetable and a few trains.
Satellite systems	See page 69.
Sports programs	Athletics heats for sports day. See PE staff for many others.
Spreadsheets	See page 74.
Stock control systems	E.g. tools in the workshop tuck in the school shop books in a small library.
Stocks and shares analysis	Don't forget to give a portion of the profits to your teacher!
Student's report project	See page 17.
Temperature monitoring program	Make sure that you have a suitable temperature sensor and interface.
Telephone directory	How about connecting it to an autodial modem! Switch over the phone when you're through.
Viewdata project	See page 67. How about setting up a system to explain how the school network works?
Weather projects	Collecting data from the school weather station. See also page 69.
Word processing	Make use of a standard letter

Writing the report

The final documentation

The time has finally arrived for you to finish your report. Did you finish the project? Does it work? Have you got any time left? You will be lucky if you have more than a couple of weeks. Writing up will be easy as you have kept a detailed diary of all the major decisions that you have made throughout the project! The most sensible approach will have been to write the reports as you go along.

Many marks have already been given to you on a **continuous assessment** basis. In other words, you have already been carefully monitored by your teachers over the last year. They will have noticed how well you have coped with problems that have arisen, checked to see if you have made good use of the school resources and monitored how much help you have been receiving etc. However, there are still many more marks to be gained from the documentation sections. Indeed these sections are often more important than the practical work on the computer.

> *Often, more marks are obtained from the documentation. It's **that** important.*

You should be aware that many projects – most, actually – do not work exactly to the specification. This does not matter too much, as many of the marks are gained during the design and analysis stage. The documentation and testing also accounts for many of the marks. You can still get a top grade even if parts of your project are not working. If professionals in industry with millions of pounds at their disposal can't get projects finished on time, it's unrealistic to expect students with more limited resources to be able to.

There is, though, a difference between not finishing on time for *genuine reasons*, and not finishing on time because you have been *lazy*. Your teachers will obviously know to which category you belong! Don't forget that your teachers mark your project. They will not be inclined to find you the maximum possible marks if you have started late, not paid attention to advice and generally wasted your time.

Let's keep it nice and neat

There is really no excuse for a computer student not producing the report on a word processor. It looks neat, your teacher and moderator can read it, and you can even get the computer to check your spelling. Don't go to the other extreme, though, of spending so long learning how to use a sophisticated desk top publishing package that you run out of time and do not complete the report. A very neat, handwritten, finished report will gain many more marks than an immaculate half-finished word processed report. Untidy handwritten reports look awful, can be hard to read and may gain fewer marks. Your teachers are usually pushed for time during the GCSE marking season and they will not spend hours trying to read and sort out your report.

Read the marking scheme

Know how your project will be marked. Don't be silly and throw marks away.

The most important advice that can be given is, please, *please*, follow the structure given in the marking scheme. This must be carried out to the letter. For example, if your scheme calls for a **title page** then put a sheet with *just* the title on it in your report. Just by doing this you have probably gained a mark already. More important, by *not* doing it you will have thrown away a very easy mark.

You must remember that your teacher and the moderator have probably got many projects to look at. They will not be very pleased if they can't find information that they need *quickly*. They may even give up trying to find information in some badly laid out reports.

It is usual to have a **contents page**. Number the pages in your report and make sure that each section that is required can be easily found.

Your board might require a contents page similar to the following example.

Contents	Page no.
Statement of the problem to be solved	2
Project specification	3
Design of solution to the problem	4
Implementation	9
Testing	15
Demonstration and evaluation	17

However, the main points to note are **follow the marking scheme** and **make sure that all the required sections are present for your particular board**.

What sort of things do we do?

This will depend on your chosen project. Everybody will be different. Even so, you will be amazed at the similarities when it comes to producing the documentation. Space will not allow us to give a completely documented project. So a simple example now follows.

Project documentation

Write the documentation for a person who will be reading it for the first time.

Take as an example the monthly financial accounts for a family. First, make sure that you have a **title** for your project. In this example, it could be 'Monthly financial statements for the home'.

Next, make sure that you state clearly what your project is intended to do. In this example, this could be as follows.

The purpose of the project

Once a month my parents get paid. The amount they get varies from one month to the next, as do all the bills that have to be paid. This project will enable a computer to keep records and print out a detailed monthly financial report for the household budget. The items to be included are as follows:

(a) Balance brought forward from previous month.

(b) Monthly income from the following sources: husband, wife and any others.

(c) The standing orders and direct debits from the bank to be included are: mortgage, loans (e.g. car or HP), insurances, rates etc.

(d) Bills split up into monthly portions such as: telephone, TV licence, car tax, water and sewage rates.

(e) Monthly expenses such as: Barclaycard and Access, petrol, food, savings, holidays etc.

(f) The balance carried forward to the next month.

The analysis of the problem

The analysis of many types of problem have been covered in detail elsewhere in this book. Assume that after a detailed study it was decided to use a **spreadsheet**.

A detailed **specification** must be drawn up. In addition, the hardware and software that you intend using must be written down in your report. The reasons why a spreadsheet was chosen must be clearly stated, and the **inputs**, **outputs** and hence the **processing** necessary must be gone into in some detail.

For this particular project the detailed layout of the screen will be very important, and a typical one is shown in Figure 8.1. Also, the **types of data** (e.g. numeric or text) and any **validation** and **verification** checks that can be carried out on the system must be covered. It will also be useful to include **structure diagrams**, **flowcharts** and any other pictorial information that can help to explain clearly your methods of solution.

Notice how the **cumulative** (running) total is updated automatically and the total income has already been calculated. This shows you some of the power of a spreadsheet. Items such as monthly standing orders need to be easy to amend because mortgage payments, for example, are variable due to changes in the interest rate.

The file structures you intend using and reasons for their choice must also be covered in detail. A simple example here would be the names of the file for each monthly account. Names such as:

MAY90, JUN90, . . . JAN91

will probably be useful as the month and year are automatically identified by the name of the file.

MONTHLY BILLS APRIL 1990

PERIOD FROM   1st April to 30th April

DETAILS	PAYMENTS	RECEIPTS	DATE	CUMULATIVE TOTAL
INCOME				
Balance B/F		67.34		67.34
Husband's income		1036.00	1st	1103.34
Wife's income		437.78	1st	1541.12
Other income		0.00		
TOTAL INCOME		1541.12		1541.12
STANDING ORDERS				
DIRECT DEBITS				
Royal Life	67.32		1st	1473.80
Abbey National	358.29		1st	1115.51
Car loan	260.12		3rd	855.39
Hire purchase	98.13		7th	757.26
Prudential	47.38		9th	709.88
Norwich Union 1	17.34		11th	692.54
Norwich Union 2	25.00		18th	667.54
Rates	42.78		21st	624.76
STAND ORDER TOTAL	916.36			624.76
MONTHLY BILLS				
Car tax	8.33			616.43
TV licence	5.33			611.10
Electricity	37.12			573.98
Telephone	18.87			555.11
Water rates	6.43			548.68
Sewage	5.87			542.81
BILL TOTAL	81.95			542.81
MONTHLY EXPENSES				
Barclaycard	67.83			474.98
Access	0.00			474.98
Food	103.27			371.71
Petrol	38.25			333.46
Savings	0.00			333.46
Etc.	217.24			116.22
EXPENSE TOTAL	426.59			116.22

BALANCE CARRIED FORWARD TO NEXT MONTH   116.22

Fig. 8.1 Financial spreadsheet on screen

You will need back-up copies in case of disaster. All this sort of information must be covered in the analysis of the problem sections.

Technical and user documentation

These important topics have not been covered in detail elsewhere in the book. In this section, the spreadsheet example will be used to consider how this sort of documentation should be produced.

User documentation

A simple manual must be written on a level appropriate to the user. This is sometimes called the **user documentation**.

It is important that no technical details are included. What is needed is an **explanation**, in the simplest possible terms, of how to use the computer to do the task of monthly accounts.

You will have already set up the spreadsheet. This would be far too complex an operation for the user. Consider now how to use the system each month.

Where to start

It makes little sense to explain how to connect the computer system together, how to format discs etc as this will have already been covered in

the computer's general manual. It is usual to start off with the assumption that the user knows how to switch on the equipment and put a disc in the drive.

After consultation with the users during the systems analysis phase the layout given in Figure 8.1 has been adopted. The example is shown complete with entries, but the initial spreadsheet for the first month would be filled with many zeros. The only things that would be filled in already are the standing orders and other things that do not change often. An example of a simple introduction is shown below.

USING THE SYSTEM

GETTING STARTED

The system has already been set up for you. An example of the screen is shown in the following picture:

MONTHLY BILLS APRIL 1990

PERIOD FROM   1st April to 30th April

DETAILS	PAYMENTS	RECEIPTS	DATE	CUMULATIVE TOTAL
INCOME				
Balance B/F		67.34		67.34
Husband's income		1036.00	1st	1103.34
Wife's income		437.78	1st	1541.12
Other income		0.00		
TOTAL INCOME		1541.12		1541.12
STANDING ORDERS DIRECT DEBITS				
Royal Life	67.32		1st	1473.80
Abbey National	358.29		1st	1115.51
Car loan	260.12		3rd	855.39
Hire purchase	98.13		7th	757.26
Prudential	47.38		9th	709.88
Norwich Union 1	17.34		11th	692.54
Norwich Union 2	25.00		18th	667.54
Rates	42.78		21st	624.76
STAND ORDER TOTAL	916.36			624.76
MONTHLY BILLS				
Car tax	8.33			616.43
TV licence	5.33			611.10
Electricity	37.12			573.98
Telephone	18.87			555.11
Water rates	6.43			548.68
Sewage	5.87			542.81
BILL TOTAL	81.95			542.81
MONTHLY EXPENSES				
Barclaycard	67.83			474.98
Access	0.00			474.98
Food	103.27			371.71
Petrol	38.25			333.46
Savings	0.00			333.46
Etc.	217.24			116.22
EXPENSE TOTAL	426.59			116.22

BALANCE CARRIED FORWARD TO NEXT MONTH   116.22

To start the system make sure that the computer is switched on and the disc labelled 'Monthly accounts' is inserted correctly into drive A.

In the following you will have to type in exactly what is asked for and then follow by pressing the RETURN KEY. Pressing the RETURN key is shown by an arrow like this: ↓

E.g. Type HELLO ↓ means type the word HELLO and press the RETURN key.

INSTRUCTIONS FOR THE BEGINNING OF EACH MONTH

The first thing to do is type SPREADSHEET ↓

The computer should respond with the screen as shown below:

ABC Computer Systems
LOCUS 123 Spreadsheet
Editing No file.
>

Next type LOAD DUMMY ↓

The computer screen should now look like this:

ABC Computer Systems
LOCUS 123 Spreadsheet
Editing DUMMY
>

Now press the ESCAPE KEY

The computer should respond with the screen as shown below:

MONTHLY BILLS DUMMY

PERIOD FROM

DETAILS	PAYMENTS	RECEIPTS	DATE	CUMULATIVE TOTAL
INCOME				
Balance B/F		0.00		0.00
Husband's income		1000.00	1st	1000.00
Wife's income		400.00	1st	1400.00
Other income		0.00		1400.00
TOTAL INCOME		1400.00		1400.00
STANDING ORDERS DIRECT DEBITS				
Royal Life	67.32		1st	1332.68
Abbey National	358.29		1st	974.39
Car loan	260.12		3rd	714.27
Hire purchase	98.13		7th	616.14
Prudential	47.38		9th	568.76
Norwich Union 1	17.34		11th	551.42
Norwich Union 2	25.00		18th	526.42
Rates	42.78		21st	483.64
STAND ORDER TOTAL	916.36			483.64
MONTHLY BILLS				
Car tax	8.33			475.31
TV licence	5.33			469.98
Electricity	37.12			432.86
Telephone	18.87			413.99
Water rates	6.43			407.56
Sewage	5.87			401.69
BILL TOTAL	81.95			401.69
MONTHLY EXPENSES				
Barclaycard	0.00			401.69
Access	0.00			401.69
Food	0.00			401.69
Petrol	0.00			401.69
Savings	0.00			401.69
Etc.	0.00			401.69
EXPENSE TOTAL	0.00			

BALANCE CARRIED FORWARD TO NEXT MONTH   401.69

First we have to change the word DUMMY to the correct month and year. To do this move the cursor over the word DUMMY by using the arrow keys, and then type in the month and year. e.g.

type APRIL 1992 ↓ if it is April 1992.

Now move the cursor over to the box to the right of PERIOD FROM and type:

1st APRIL to 30th APRIL (or the appropriate period)

Move the cursor by using the arrow keys on the keyboard until it is over the box showing the balance brought forward from last month. Look at your bank statement and decide how much you had left over last month. (In future the spreadsheet will tell you!)

Next type in the amount. E.g.

type 67.34 ↓

Move the cursor over the HUSBAND'S INCOME box and type in the income for this month. E.g.

type 1036.00 ↓

Now move the cursor over the WIFE'S INCOME box and type in the income for this month. E.g.

type 437.78 ↓

The top half of the screen (using the above figures) should now look like this:

MONTHLY BILLS APRIL 1992

PERIOD FROM   1st April to 30th April

DETAILS	PAYMENTS	RECEIPTS	DATE	CUMULATIVE TOTAL
INCOME				
Balance B/F		67.34		67.34
Husband's income		1036.00	1st	1103.34
Wife's income		437.78	1st	1541.12
Other income		0.00		
TOTAL INCOME		1541.12		1541.12

Alter any other figures using the same methods as above.

Finally, fill in the monthly expenses in the same way.

WHAT NEXT?

Whatever you do don't switch off or go away to have a cup of tea!

YOU MUST FIRST SAVE THE INFORMATION ON DISC.

To do this press the ESCAPE key. The screen should now look like this:

ABC Computer Systems
LOCUS 123 Spreadsheet
Editing DUMMY

>

You must decide on a file name. If the month is April and the year is 1992 then a good name would be APR92. If this was your choice of name then you would type:

SAVE APR92 ↓

Next catalogue your disc to make sure that the file is there.

Finally, place the disc marked 'Monthly accounts backup' into the drive and repeat the saving method shown above. This makes an identical copy on another disc which should be stored in a different place to the original for safekeeping.

GETTING A PRINTOUT

If you are starting from scratch then load the spreadsheet by typing:

SPREADSHEET ↓

Next load the file you wish to print by typing:

LOAD APR92 ↓ or whatever file name you have chosen.

Make sure that the printer is connected and switched on. You must now type:

PRINT ↓

A copy of the screen should now appear on the printer and should be filed for safe keeping and future reference.

That's all it takes

The above is obviously not complete, but gives an idea of the sort of approach to take when dealing with user documentation. Don't forget that you must convince the moderator that it works. Therefore you will need printouts of the screen as the program is running.

Technical or program documentation

This is not intended for the user of the system. For the purpose of the GCSE project the first consideration *must* be to enable the teacher and moderator to understand it!

The planning and problem analysis stages together with your structure diagrams and flowcharts form a major part of the technical documentation. The style you use will depend on whether you have written a program or used a package.

Assume that you have chosen to solve your problem by writing your own software. The technical documentation for one board is summarized in the following list.

1 Outline or macro flowcharts and/or structure diagrams
(or equivalents)

2 Description of the programming methods used
(e.g. the user interface, validation, verification checks etc)

3 Input/output file formats
(e.g. a list of all the data formats and the internal and external data structures etc)

4 Program testing
(This is to include the reasons for the choice of test data and test runs on the systems etc)

5 Annotated listings
(Listings of the programs with explanations and comments)

6 Output demonstrating that the program works
(This could be in the form of printout, photos, audio or video tape recordings)

Make it easy to understand

When designing technical documentation, explain your project so that a fellow student can easily understand it. This is often difficult for students to do, especially the clever ones! They seem to delight in writing complex programs that no one can understand. This is *not* useful and will **lose you marks**. By all means make use of clever routines, but write them in such a way that other people can understand what's going on. Aim for simplicity.

Now assume that you have chosen to solve your problem by making use of one or more software packages. This time much of the technical documentation will be different. You will probably have to make sure that it includes the following details.

1 A full description of the solution indicating clearly both the hardware and software that was used. (In addition to this you will need to describe the user interface.)

2 Suitable methods of data capture, validation, verification and storage

3 Evidence that your system (where necessary) can:

- create records
- output records
- search for records

> *You must provide evidence that your project works.*

- sort records
- insert/amend/delete record

4 Evidence that your system has been tested together with an explanation of the reasons for the choice of test data

Don't forget unusual as well as usual data.

5 Proof that the system can be used in a realistic way in the form of hard copy, or other evidence such as suitably annotated listings (This means show the output but write extra notes to explain what is happening. See the spreadsheet example in this section.)

The above are general points. You must make sure that you follow the correct procedures laid down by your own examinations board. Make sure that your teacher explains it to you before you write up the project.

Finally . . .

Evaluation and possible improvements

No project is ever perfect, but after spending many months developing your project, the least you should be able to do is say how it could be improved. This is usually easy with the benefit of hindsight.

One thing that you must *not* do is to alter your original specification in the light of what you have learnt while developing the project. Some boards prevent you from doing this by actually getting the teacher to mark your method of solution *before* you are allowed to develop and test the system. This may sound tough, but is actually what happens in industry. Here the systems analysts would prepare the specifications and the general methods to be used. They would not expect the programmers to alter the specifications at a later date unless they had good reasons.

If you do find ways of improving the system then this is what should be written down in the improvements section. Make a note of these possible improvements in your diary as it may be a couple of months before you will write these reasons in your report.

Advice about coursework

Be in the know!

It is wise to be aware of what is expected of you before starting your coursework. Knowing these simple facts will enable you to avoid the pitfalls which many students seem to find. Also, it will enable you to carry out your work with greater confidence. Try to appreciate what is being done by your teacher over the year, and also the roles that the moderator and teachers play in assessing your final grade.

What you should know

What are they looking for?

A quick summary

Your teachers will need to be shown that you can use a computer system sensibly to solve an appropriate problem that you have chosen. In addition to this, you must be able to produce the documentation.

They will be looking to see if you can choose the right hardware and software packages that lead to an efficient solution to your problem. If your problem requires the use of a programming language, they will be checking that you have written it in a sensible way.

The relationships between you, your teacher and the moderator

It is your teacher's responsibility to assess the work that you do over the year and decide on the probable mark that you will be awarded. When all the marks have been awarded by your teacher, some or all of the projects from your school will be sent off for moderation. This means that they will be compared to similar projects from other schools all over the country. This is the job of the moderator and is designed to get over the problem of having a teacher who marks too hard or too easily.

The teacher's main role in marking your project

It is obviously good if you like and get on well with your teacher, but there is really very little scope for influencing the outcome of your grade other

than by working hard and doing well. This is because of the strict **criteria** (things to be achieved) laid down by the examination boards.

There is usually a **marking scheme** that is used for the coursework and you should make sure that you are familiar with the main points of it. The marking scheme for each board will be slightly different.

Your teachers will have very detailed reasons for awarding marks for your project. For example, if they were finding out if you have chosen and used appropriate data for your project, then they may mark according to the following:

Grade G   You are able to use data that you have been given to test your algorithms.

Grade E/F   You are able to choose simple data to test simple algorithms.

etc.

Or to get a grade A:

It often helps to appreciate what is needed to get a particular grade.

Grade A   You are able to choose and justify your choice of data to test your algorithms.

The above are called **grade related criteria** because they relate what you can do with the grade that you will get.

You can appreciate what sort of effort is likely to result in a particular grade. This does not mean that you can predict the exact grade that you should get, but it can and indeed does give an outline of the achievements necessary to be within certain grade boundaries.

You can use the following as a rough guide for the whole project.

Grade F

Students would have attempted only a very simple problem and have solved it making use of a pre-written software package.

The testing of the solution to the problem would only cover the very obvious aspects of the system, and the student would have been given the test data. The documentation would be of poor quality.

Grade C

Students would have attempted a substantial problem and solved it reasonably well.

The system does not fully work but many sub-systems have been successfully tested. All important aspects of the project have been tested.

Students should be able to identify some limitations of their system and be able to suggest some improvements to it.

The methods of solution need not be efficient but the documentation of the project should be of a quality such that it enables an intelligent reader to follow the methods of solution with relative ease.

Grade A

Students would have attempted a substantial project which is successful in the most important aspects or completely working.

Students should have developed efficient methods of solution and the standard of documentation would be high, enabling an intelligent reader to follow easily the solution to the problem.

Don't worry too much about your project if you have worked hard and produced some results.

The students would have probably investigated several methods of solution and justified their choice with appropriate technical reasons.

The system would be extensively tested in all the obvious and not so obvious cases. Where possible these tests will be backed up by documentary evidence.

The performance of the system will have been fully evaluated and where improvements are necessary suggestions for implementing these improvements will have been given.

Never over estimate the importance of project work

Don't forget that in most syllabuses the *majority* of the marks come from the *written examination* in combination with the *case study* if appropriate. However, projects must be done. Failure to do them may result in being judged absent from the exam even if you do brilliantly during the written exam.

How much help do I get at the start?

It is usual for your teachers to give much help and advice when it comes to choosing a suitable project. This is because they have much experience in solving similar problems and know many of the pitfalls months before you will encounter them. Your teacher will give advice and guidance and discuss with you possible general methods of solution. This help given will not penalize your final mark in any way whatsoever.

What about help during the project?

Once you have started your project you are expected to do most of the work on your own. You will obviously have to ask teachers and friends for their advice and opinions, but you must not expect your teachers or your friends to do most of the work for you. It is very easy for a teacher to identify work that is beyond the general standard that a student usually displays in class.

When your project is finished your teachers will have to sign a declaration saying that to the best of their knowledge your project is all your own work except for the help already recorded.

What if I get stuck?

There will probably be occasions when you can't continue without extra help. Your teacher will obviously not leave you in this state for too long or you will never finish the project. It is a requirement of the system that your teacher must record any major help given during the project. Here we are not talking about the quick prod, suggestion or nudge in the right direction. We are talking about major help such as developing an algorithm for you or having to help you every time you get a bug in your program.

A system of **scaling** operates on many computer studies syllabuses. This means that your overall marks are scaled down according to how much help you have received. If you have received no help at all or only received occasional help and tips then your **scaling factor** will obviously be 100 per cent. If on the other hand you can never get on by yourself or without the constant help of friends, your scaling factor will be very much lower.

Different standards of projects

Some people seem to do easy projects, compared to others in the class. This is quite obvious and necessary as there will be some students who have more ability than others.

It's very difficult to be original. Choose a sensible problem and solve it to the best of your ability.

A scaling factor is often applied reflecting the difficulty of the project. Very easy and obvious projects requiring little thought will be marked down, compared to more difficult and demanding projects. Don't go too far the other way and choose a project that is too difficult. An unfinished difficult project will not score as many marks as a completely finished, well-documented, good standard project. It is important that you listen carefully to the advice of your teacher at the beginning.

For example, suppose that you have a very simple working project on which you have been given much help. After being marked using the mark scheme you may be awarded 90 per cent. However, a scaling factor of 25 per cent might be applied and therefore, your actual mark would be:

$0.25 \times 90 = 22.5\%$

How original must it be?

With tens of thousands of computer studies students, it is very difficult if not almost impossible to come up with something that no one has done before. It would be foolish to attempt a project that someone else is doing in the same school in the same year. However, projects done in the past at the same school are often done better in future years by students who did not even know the project had been done previously.

You must under no circumstances copy programs out of magazines and books to submit them as your own. This not only infringes copyright but will get you nowhere if your teacher finds out. (They most usually do, either by instinct or through some supergrass in the class! Don't forget that people who have struggled with their projects will feel cheated and think that you have an unfair advantage.) *You will probably be required to sign a form that states that the project is entirely your own work.* Imagine your embarrassment if your work is found out to be a copy of someone else's by the examination board during moderation!

You must realize that it is acceptable to copy programs and routines from books and magazines if they are to form **a small sub-section** of your project. For example, you may need an efficient routine to sort names into order and this would only form a small section of your project. Then you can use one of the standard methods from a book. You **must** remember to quote the book or magazine article in the **bibliography** section of your project. You will not be penalized at all for sensible use of reference material in this way.

What questions should I ask my teacher?

Most teachers will spend several lessons discussing how to approach the coursework component of the course. Even so, it is useful to have a list of questions to ask your teacher, just to ensure that all the important things you need to know have been covered. A typical list of questions now follows.

1 Do I have to do a single major project or several small ones?
(Some boards prefer a couple of smaller projects on different aspects of computers.)

2 What is the percentage mark allocated to the project work?
(Don't forget that some syllabuses have a **case study** in addition to the practical project and written examination.)

3 How much time have I got to do the project?

4 What is the deadline date for handing in the project?
(Usually April/May in the year of the written exam.)

5 May I have a detailed copy of the mark scheme that will be used to mark the projects?

6 How many A4 pages should the project take?
(This usually excludes any computer output.)

7 Can I make use of photographs, audio tape and video tape?

8 Can you explain how much assistance you are allowed to give? (If possible, get them to give some examples.)

Glossary of project terms

When reading through the book you will have been aware that some of the terms used might be difficult to understand, for example, **algorithm**, **user interface**, **annotated listing** etc. The following glossary is intended to help with these technical project terms. It is *not* intended as a complete glossary for your computer studies course.

In the glossary you will find many words in *italics*. This means that these words are *also* in the glossary. Therefore, if you are looking up the meaning of a term and come across a word in *italics* that you can't understand, then this too can be looked up in the glossary.

Glossary

> *Make sure you understand all the technical terms.*

Algorithm. A process or set of rules for solving a problem.

Analysis. Can refer to several stages of your project, e.g. the *systems analysis* phase, analysis of the results (seeing if the results are correct etc).

Annotated listing. A listing with comments and explanations to show how a program works.

Applications package. See *software package*.

Assembly language. A low level language designed for a specific type of processor. Not recommended for GCSE projects unless part of your project really needs it. For example, very fast *data capture* when using a *control project*.

BASIC. Beginner's All-purpose Symbolic Instruction Code. A popular high level language used for computer studies projects at school. Make sure your programs are well *structured*.

Buggy. A small simple robot connected to the computer.

CAD (computer aided design). A *software package* that enables you easily to produce engineering or architect-type drawings. The output is usually on a plotter. Good projects can be produced on these systems.

Case study. A detailed study of specific computer applications such as airlines or estate agents. It is not the same as the *project*, although it may be part of your *coursework*.

COMAL. A *structured* high level language similar in some ways to *BASIC*.

Control project. A *project* that involves the use of the computer to *control* an electronic device such as a *buggy* or weather station etc.

Coursework. This is sometimes the same as your *project* but most boards require that a *case study* is also undertaken.

Data. Numbers, names etc that form the raw material to be entered into the computer system, e.g. the results of a survey.

Database. A sophisticated system which allows you to build up files of information and extract the information from them in a variety of ways. It is very much easier to use them than to attempt to write your own file handling software.

Data capture. The methods by which data is collected. This could include entry direct into the computer or on *data capture forms*.

Data capture forms. Forms specially designed for the purpose of gathering data for entry into a computer system. You may have to design these special forms (or screens) for your project.

Default values. A set of standard values which remain the same unless the *user* changes them.

Design. The parts of your *project* where you are designing solutions to the various problems, e.g. producing flowcharts etc. This is often referred to as *analysis and design*.

Desk top publishing system. This is a *software package* designed to produce newspaper type documents. i.e. different type styles and pictures. It is much more sophisticated than a *word processor*.

Diary. See *project diary*.

Documentation. The reports (writing and diagrams etc) that go with your project. Both *user documentation* and *technical documentation* must be present in your *project report*.

File structure. The way in which your files are to be organized in your project, i.e. details of records and fields etc.

Hardware. The computer system that you are using, i.e. type of computer, printers etc. You must list the hardware that you use for your project.

Implementation. The way that things are carried out, e.g. you might have implemented a checking procedure for data entry.

Information retrieval package. This is usually a simple type of *database*. This package will allow you to create a simple system to retrieve information from your computer, e.g. an address book system.

Input. This is all the *data* that your system needs to operate, the checks that you will carry out on the data and the types of data etc.

Interactive video system. Hardware and software that enables the computer to control a *laser disc player*.

Integrated software packages. These are generally groups of *software packages* such as *databases, word processors, spreadsheets, graph plotting packages* etc that can easily pass *data* between themselves, e.g. the graph package could print a graph of information contained in the spreadsheet.

Interface. The boundary between two systems. Commonly used in *control projects* to indicate the ways in which connections are made to the computer. See also *user interface*.

Interview. A meeting, usually with the person or people who will be using your project. Its aim is to sort out the best way to get things done. Several interviews are usually needed.

Laser disc player. A player capable of replaying the video and audio information stored on a laser disc.

Manual. The instruction book.

Marking scheme. The detailed set of instructions from the examination board showing how your project is to be marked. Your teacher should have copies of the marking schemes.

MIDI. Musical Instrument Digital Interface.

Moderator. The person, usually a teacher from another school, who checks the marking and standards etc of the projects from your school. This ensures that national standards are maintained.

Moderation. The process of checking the *coursework* by the moderators.

Network. Computers connected together to share information and resources such as printers and disc drives.

Oscilloscope. An electronic instrument with a cathode ray tube designed to show pictures of electrical signals.

Output. This is all the *data* that you expect to extract from your system once the *processing* has been done. It usually includes the layout of the data with typical examples showing that your system is working.

Package. See *software package*.

Pascal. A high level programming language designed to aid *structured programming*.

Processing. All the things that have to be done with the *input* to provide the appropriate output, i.e. the main processing which lies at the heart of your project. It is usual to include things like *file structure* etc.

Project. The practical coursework intended to demonstrate that you can make sensible use of a computer system to solve an appropriate problem.

Project diary. A simple account of all the major decisions that you have made while doing your project. It makes the write-up and *documentation* so much easier to do.

Project report. The written report that must accompany your project.

Project supervisor. Usually your teacher.

Satellite system. A system that enables computers to extract live data from some satellite broadcasts.

Software. The programs that accompany your project. If you have no programs then you will be using a *software package* to solve your project.

Software package. Sometimes called a *package*. This is the name given to the *word processors*, *databases*, *spreadsheets*, *CAD* systems, etc that have been written by the computer companies to do specific tasks. You may use one or more of these for your *project*.

Specification. The technical details explaining exactly what the *project* is to do.

Spreadsheet. A system of rows and columns of cells which help you to work out related figures with ease. This system is to an accountant what a word processor is to a secretary.

Structured programming. Techniques making use of procedures, use of loops such as while, repeat until, etc and the use of meaningful variable names etc which make the programs much easier to read and understand.

Systems analysis. The phase in which you investigate a problem to see if it is going to be suitable for solution by a computer.

Systems analyst. The person who looks at the problem to see how it may be best solved by using a computer. In your GCSE *project* this is you!

Technical documentation. The *documentation* that explains in technical detail how your project works. It should enable people to understand your project easily and modify it if necessary.

Test data. The *data* used for getting known results from a system. Also, the data used to check the *verification* and *validation* methods.

Testing. It is essential that your project (or at least the parts that work!) be fully tested using valid *test data*.

User. The person who will use your project.

User documentation. The (mostly non-technical) description that enables the *user* easily to use the project that you have designed. It is often in the form of a simple *manual*.

User friendly. If your system is easy and obvious to use then it is called *user friendly*. You must aim to make your project as user friendly as possible.

User interface. What the *user* of the system sees when they are using the computer, i.e. the means of communication between the *user* and the computer system.

Validation. Testing *data* to see if it is valid, e.g. the maximum height allowed might be two metres.

Verification. Testing *data* to see if it has been entered correctly. Not so easy to do with the limited resources at school.

Videos. Useful for showing animated sequences, however, make sure they are in VHS format unless otherwise stated.

Viewdata. Information in the form obtained from Prestel and teletext services.

Voltmeter. An electronic instrument used to measure voltage.

Word processor. A software package that turns your computer into a dedicated text processing machine. You should try to write your project using a word processor.

APPENDIX

Syllabus analysis

London & East Anglian Group (LEAG)

Students are entered for the GCSE at three different levels. A, B and C. These are as follows:

Level A (grades D – G)	Paper 1	1½ hours duration	Written paper	35%
	Paper 2	2 hours duration	Case study	35%
		– – – – –	Project	30%
Level B (grades C – F)	Paper 3	1½ hours duration	Written paper	35%
	Paper 4	2 hours duration	Case study	35%
		– – – – –	Project	30%
Level C (grades A – F)	Paper 3	1½ hours duration	Written paper	35% of 75%
	Paper 4	2 hours duration	Case study	35% of 75%
		– – – – –	Project	30% of 75%
	Paper 5	1½ hours duration	Written paper	25%

Midland Examining Group (MEG)

(As from 1990)

Paper 1	45 minutes duration	Written paper	
Paper 2	75 minutes duration	Written paper	} 50%
Paper 3	1 hour duration	Written paper	

You must take at least one but *not* more than two of papers 1, 2 and 3. The best marks will be used to determine the grade.

Case study	1 hour duration	$16\frac{2}{3}$%
Project		$33\frac{1}{3}$%

Papers 1, 2 and 3 relate to grades as follows:

Grade G   Grade F   Grade E   Grade D   Grade C   Grade B   Grade A
←————————paper 1————————→   ←————paper 2————→   ←————paper 3————→

Northern Examination Association (NEA)

Paper 1	(30%)	Written paper
Paper 2	(30%)	Written paper

Case study. Reference will be made to the case study in the written examination papers.

Project Work (40%)

This will be marked in two sections:

● analysis and design stage   (20%)
● implementation and testing stage   (20%)

Southern Examining Group (SEG)

Paper 1	45 minutes duration	Objective test	20%
Paper 2	1½ hours duration	Written paper	30%
Paper 3	1 hour duration	Written paper	20%
Paper 4	– – – – –	Project	30%

Welsh Joint Education Committee (WJEC)

Paper 1	2 hours duration	Written paper
Paper 2	1½ hours duration	Written paper
Paper 3	2 hours duration	Written paper
Papers 1 and 2	(Easier option) 70%	Grades C, D, E, F and G
Papers 3 and 2	(Harder option) 70%	Grades A, B, C, D and E

For the easier option the marks are:

Paper 1	40%
Paper 2	30%
Project	30%

For the harder options the marks are:

Paper 2	30%
Paper 3	40%
Project	30%

At the time of writing all information about syllabus requirements was correct. However, because syllabus requirements change, you must **always** check with your examination group or your teacher before you start any coursework to make sure that you are going what is required.

Examination groups: addresses

LEAG – London and East Anglian Group

London   University of London Schools Examinations Board
              Stewart House, 32 Russell Square, London WC1B 5DN

LREB   London Regional Examinations Board
              Lyon House, 104 Wandsworth High Street, London SW18 4LF

EAEB   East Anglian Examinations Board
              The Lindens, Lexden Road, Colchester, Essex CO3 3RL (0206 549595)

MEG – Midlands Examining Group

Cambridge   University of Cambridge Local Examinations Syndicate
              Syndicate Buildings, 1 Hills Road, Cambridge CB1 2EU (0223 61111)

O & C   Oxford and Cambridge Schools Examinations Board
              10 Trumpington Street, Cambridge CB2 1QB and Elsfield Way,
              Oxford OX2 8EP

SUJB   Southern Universities' Joint Board for School Examinations
              Cotham Road, Bristol BS6 6DD

WMEB   West Midlands Examinations Board
              Norfolk House, Smallbrook Queensway, Birmingham B5 4NJ

EMREB   East Midlands Regional Examinations Board
              Robins Wood House, Robins Wood Road, Aspley, Nottingham NG8 3NH

NEA – Northern Examination Association (*write to your local board.*)

JMB   Joint Matriculation Board (061-273 2565)
              Devas Street, Manchester M15 6EU (*also for centres outside the NEA area*)

ALSEB   Associated Lancashire Schools Examining Board
              12 Harter Street, Manchester M1 6HL

NREB   North Regional Examinations Board
              Wheatfield Road, Westerhope, Newcastle upon Tyne NE5 5JZ

NWREB   North-West Regional Examinations Board
              Orbit House, Albert Street, Eccles, Manchester M30 0WL

YHREB   Yorkshire and Humberside Regional Examinations Board
              Harrogate Office — 31 – 33 Springfield Avenue, Harrogate HG1 2HW
              Sheffield Office — Scarsdale House, 136 Derbyshire Lane, Sheffield S8 8SE

NISEC – Northern Ireland

NISEC   Northern Ireland Schools Examinations Council
              Beechill House, 42 Beechill Road, Belfast BT8 4RS (0232 704666)

SEB – Scotland

SEB   Scottish Examinations Board
              Ironmills Road, Dalkeith, Midlothian EH22 1BR (031-663 6601)

SEG – Southern Examining Group

AEB   The Associated Examining Board
              Stag Hill House, Guildford, Surrey GU2 5XJ (0483 503123)

Oxford   Oxford Delegacy of Local Examinations
              Ewert Place, Summertown, Oxford OX2 7BZ

SREB   Southern Regional Examinations Board
              Eastleigh House, Market Street, Eastleigh, Hampshire SO5 4SW

SEREB   South-East Regional Examinations Board
              Beloe House, 2 – 10 Mount Ephraim Road, Tunbridge Wells TN1 1EU

SWEB   South-Western Examinations Board
              23 – 29 Marsh Street, Bristol BS1 4BP

WJEC – Wales

WJEC   Welsh Joint Education Committee
              245 Western Avenue, Cardiff CF5 2YX (0222 561231)

(The boards to which you should write are underlined in each case.)

INDEX